Praise for *Last Things First*

"By offering some wonderful insights into the four last things (death, judgment, heaven, and hell), Regis Flaherty shows us how to refine our focus on the things of this life and how to prepare well for the joys of eternal life."

James J. Drummey
Author of *Catholic Replies* and *Catholic Replies 2*
(C.R. Publications)

"Business consultants and life coaches tell us that we should begin our tasks with an end in mind. That's no news to Christians. Tradition teaches us to live life that way. If all our tasks have everlasting consequences, then we'd better keep those four ends in mind: death, judgment, heaven, and hell. Regis Flaherty has given us a practical plan for living well, in a book that's a joy to read."

Mike Aquilina
Author and EWTN host
Vice President, St. Paul Center for Biblical Theology

"It's absolutely of first priority that Catholics today have a clear, eternal perspective on the meaning and purpose of life, and most importantly, how it ends. Regis Flaherty has done a valuable service in helping Catholics appropriate this eternal perspective as an indispensable aid for making wise decisions in everyday life."

Ralph Martin
Director, Graduate Theology Programs in Evangelization
Sacred Heart Major Seminary, Archdiocese of Detroit

"I knew I could count on Rege Flaherty to take a tough subject and make a solid and clearly Catholic presentation. Rege Flaherty makes the case for a Catholic understanding of the 'last things.' Read *Last Things First* for one essential reason: if death makes no sense, nothing makes sense."

Robert P. Lockwood
Former president and publisher of Our Sunday Visitor
Author of *A Faith for Grown-Ups:*
A Midlife Conversation About What Really Matters
(Loyola Press)

Last Things
FIRST

Last Things FIRST

Regis J. Flaherty

Our Sunday Visitor Publishing Division
Our Sunday Visitor, Inc
Huntington, Indiana 46750

Nihil Obstat:
Rev. Daniel J. Maurer, S.T.L.
Censor Librorum

Imprimatur:
✠ Donald W. Wuerl
Bishop of Pittsburgh
June 6, 2005

The *nihil obstat* and *imprimatur* are declarations that a work is free from doctrinal or moral error. It is not implied that those who have granted the *nihil obstat* and *imprimatur* agree with the contents, opinions, or statements expressed.

The Scripture citations contained in this work are taken from the *Catholic Edition of the Revised Standard Version of the Bible* (RSV), copyright © 1965 and 1966 by the Division of Christian Education of the National Council of the Churches of Christ in the United States of America. Used by permission. All rights reserved.

Selections from the *Catechism of the Catholic Church, Second Edition,* for use in the United States of America, copyright © 1994 and 1997, United States Catholic Conference — Libreria Editrice Vaticana. Used by permission. All rights reserved.

Excerpts from the English translation of *Order of Christian Funerals,* © 1985, International Committee on English in the Liturgy, Inc. All rights reserved.

Every reasonable effort has been made to determine copyright holders of excerpted materials and to secure permissions as needed. If any copyrighted materials have been inadvertently used in this work without proper credit being given in one form or another, please notify Our Sunday Visitor in writing so that future printings of this work may be corrected accordingly.

Our Sunday Visitor Publishing Division
Our Sunday Visitor, Inc.
200 Noll Plaza
Huntington, IN 46750

ISBN: 1-59276-133-X (Inventory No. T184)
LCCN: 2005931299

Cover design by Troy Lefevra
Interior design by Sherri L. Hoffman

PRINTED IN THE UNITED STATES OF AMERICA

This book is dedicated to the members of my family who have already gone to their eternal reward, especially my Dad, Rege, my sister, Patty, and my brother, Kevin. In this life their love and example inspired me. May their prayers now sustain me.

CONTENTS

ABBREVIATIONS

Old Testament

Genesis — Gen
Exodus — Ex
Leviticus —Lev
Numbers — Num
Deuteronomy — Deut
Joshua — Josh
Judges — Judg
Ruth — Ruth
1 Samuel — 1 Sam
2 Samuel — 2 Sam
1 Kings — 1 Kings
2 Kings — 2 Kings
1 Chronicles — 1 Chron
2 Chronicles — 2 Chron
Ezra — Ezra
Nehemiah — Neh
Tobit — Tob
Judith — Jud
Esther — Esther
1 Maccabees — 1 Mac
2 Maccabees — 2 Mac
Job — Job
Psalms — Ps
Proverbs — Prov
Ecclesiastes — Eccles
Song of Solomon — Song
Canticles — Cant
Wisdom — Wis
Sirach — Sir
Isaiah — Is

Jeremiah — Jer
Lamentations — Lam
Baruch — Bar
Ezekial — Ezek
Daniel — Dan
Hosea — Hos
Joel — Joel
Amos — Amos
Jonah — Jon
Micah — Mic
Nahum — Nah
Habakkuk — Hab
Zephaniah — Zeph
Haggai — Hag
Zechariah — Zech
Malachi — Mal

New Testament

Matthew — Mt
Mark — Mk
Luke — Lk
John — Jn
Acts of the Apostles — Acts
Romans — Rom
1 Corinthians — 1 Cor
2 Corinthians — 2 Cor
Galatians — Gal
Ephesians — Eph
Philippians — Phil
Colossians — Col
1 Thessalonians — 1 Thess

2 Thessalonians — 2 Thess

1 Timothy — 1 Tim

2 Timothy — 2 Tim

Titus — Tit

Philemon — Philem

Hebrews — Heb

James — Jas

1 Peter — 1 Pet

2 Peter — 2 Pet

1 John — 1 Jn

2 John — 2 Jn

3 John — 3 Jn

Jude — Jude

Revelation — Rev

Church Documents

CCC — *Catechism of the Catholic Church, Second Edition*, United States Catholic Conference, ©1994 and 1997.

EV — *Evangelium Vitae* (The Gospel of Life), John Paul II, March 25, 1995.

OCF — *Order of Christian Funerals*, approved by the National Conference of Catholic Bishops for use in the diocese of the United States of America, 14 November 1985. Confirmed by decree of the Congregation for Divine Worship, 20 April 1987.

PREFACE

It is not often that an author can boast that he has written a book with universal appeal. A central theme in this book is death — surely a universal phenomenon. Everyone reading this book will face it. Most men and women will also face the death of some of those whom they love.

But perhaps I have used one incorrect word. Universal is correct, but appeal is certainly open for discussion. For, in most conversations, death is a topic without much appeal. In fact, it is a topic that is generally avoided. Yet as Christians we believe that Christ has conquered death through His life, death, and resurrection. If we are found in Him, then we have no need to fear death. We can proclaim with St. Paul: "Death is swallowed up in victory. O death, where is thy victory? O death, where is thy sting?" (1 Cor 15:54-55).

In this book, I invite you to break with the polite convention of our society and discuss reality that has eternal consequences — death: its meaning, the issues that surround it, how we prepare for it, and what we can expect after it. Let's explore mortality from a Catholic perspective. Viewing death with the eyes of the Church and her Savior makes a world of difference in how we live the days of our earthly life. It literally changes the way we look at our world and at those who live in it. Let's look at the "last things" first so that we will have an accurate grasp of reality — so that we can live this life with an eternal perspective. And in that we will find hope and freedom.

"Make up your mind to use death as we are supposed to. It can lift our eyes to eternity."[1]

INTRODUCTION

When you read a mystery novel or watch a suspense movie, the story unfolds slowly. You wonder how it will end: "Who is the murderer? What do the clues mean?" When you reach the end of the story, all that you have previously read or seen begins to make sense. Knowing the end brings clarity to the rest of the story.

Our lives are stories that are slowly unfolding. We often wonder about the "why" of the various people and events that impact our lives. We question: "Why is there suffering? Why can't I resolve this problem in my life? How can I best care for those I love? How should I live my life? Where should I focus my time and energy? Does what I do make a difference? Do I make a difference?" If we knew the end, the answers to many of these questions would become clearer. In fact, if we knew the end, it could help us to "write the story" of our lives. Many of life's mysteries would be solved, or at least placed in perspective, if we know the facts about the end.

Consideration of the "final things" has always had an important place in Catholic thinking and spirituality. The traditional Catholic retreat often included a reflection on the last things — death, judgment, heaven, and hell. By thinking of the aspects of life's end, the retreatant was to gain clarity for living. That annual retreat was an opportunity for the retreatant to adjust his or her perspective. Taking a sober look at death and the subsequent realities could change the way the person lived his or her life.

Fr. Benedict Groeschel has written, "Death is a powerful teacher and has many lessons to teach us. Learn from death that nothing in this world lasts forever.... Learn from death not to cling to anything in such a way that you can't go on without it.

Instead, learn to refer all things to eternity. Do not be so comfortable with anything in this world that you will be unprepared to leave it."[2] Because thinking of one's death puts life in perspective, many saints made it a daily practice, usually as part of their morning prayer. St. Francis of Assisi encouraged his followers to often think about death for it would help them meditate on their salvation rather than on what is passing and transitory. St. Thérèse of Lisieux, known as the Little Flower, lived her short life with zest and joy. She writes in her autobiography, *Story of a Soul,* that she regularly contemplated her death and the life thereafter. When she was asked upon what she reflected during mental prayer, she responded: "I think about God, about the shortness of life, about eternity."[3]

This eternal perspective — knowing that the goal of this life is eternal life with the Trinity — helps an individual order his life in such a way that he will reach that goal. It also encourages a person to set his mind "on things that are above, not on things that are on earth" (Col 3:2).

An athlete may post a picture of an Olympic gold medal winner on her mirror, so that she will see it every morning. That reminder helps her to keep focus on the prize that she most desires. Or a man may post a personal note on the refrigerator door to serve as a regular reminder that to get into the physical shape that he desires, he needs, at times, to refrain from some food. If in the spiritual life we keep our goal in view, it will help us to live a holy and godly life. We can then attain not a perishable crown but an imperishable, eternal one (cf. 1 Cor 9:25). We can get into spiritual shape that will allow us to run to obtain the prize that is promised those who are faithful in following Christ (cf. 1 Cor 9:24; Phil 3:14).

In a world filled with so many distractions, it is easy to get lost and wander from the right path. If someone is hiking through a forest to a distant hill, the hiker could easily be lost amid the many trees and shrubs. But if he stops occasionally and looks to the horizon, he will see the top of the hill rising above the tallest trees. He then gets his orientation and begins the hike again with the knowledge that he is heading in the right direction.

Spiritually, Christians need to keep their eyes on the horizon. It is easy to go astray in the forest of life that surrounds us. The demands of the immediate — responsibilities of family, employment, and social life — easily keep the body and the mind occupied. But the things of this earthly life are passing away. Daily the ephemeral loudly calls to each person, but here we have no lasting home. We are to "seek the things that are above, where Christ is, seated at the right hand of God" (Col 3:1b).

In that quest to keep a good focus, I have divided this book into four sections. In Section I, we will reflect on the "last things." What exactly is it — the prize — for which we strive? What do we know about the eternal life that is spoken of in the Scriptures and taught by the Church? Is it something worth our efforts?

Next, in Section II, we will discuss our lives in the here and now. If there is a life that we do well to seek, what are the means to attain it? How must we live today so that we position ourselves to best enter the life hereafter? What tools, exercises, and aids are available to us for reaching that goal?

There is then a necessary transition between this life and the next life. That is the topic for Section III. What comes between the now and the then — between the here and the there? How do we bridge the gap between this mortal reality and the immortal reality?

The final things of this life, including death, don't often get discussed in polite company. Yet few things impact the individual, family, and society as does death. Death is unavoidable and, if it does not make sense, then nothing makes sense. Alternatively, if death fits into our perspective on life and if we can find joy and peace because we see in death a breaking of chains and the entrance into a life that makes all else pale, we truly have good news that is worth sharing. That sharing is the topic for Section IV, the final section of this book.

It is my hope that in reading this book you will begin to see that there is good news to be found in reflecting on death and on what comes before and, most importantly, what comes after. So let us discard the polite convention and explore ultimate reality — the last things.

What else is time but the medium through which we move from here to heaven?

Regis Martin, *What Is the Church?*
(Steubenville, OH: Emmaus Road, 2003), p. 23

FOR PERSONAL CONSIDERATION

1. Do I ever think of my death and of the life to follow? When? How often?

2. When someone close to me died, how did it affect me? How did I handle my grieving? In what did I find consolation?

3. Do I find meaning in this life because of my belief in the next life? How does that belief affect my day to day activities? My relationship with others?

SECTION I

⁓

The Last Things

**"LORD, let me know my end,
and what is the measure of my days;
let me know how fleeting my life is!"**

Ps 39:4

CHAPTER 1

The Last Things

Eighty-one percent of Americans believe that there is some sort of an afterlife. Another nine percent think that there may be an afterlife, but just aren't sure. Meanwhile, ten percent are convinced that there is no life after death.[4] Surely some people will be surprised when they die!

According to the same survey, seventy-six percent of respondents said that there is a heaven, while a slightly lower percentage, seventy-one percent, believe that there is a hell.

If there are realities that exist on the other side of the grave, shouldn't these spiritual realities form our earthly life? After all, seventy-one percent believe that there is a hell. Those who expressed that belief identified hell as a "separation from God's presence" or as "a place of torment and suffering." Even those who didn't express any substantial understanding of the nature of hell agreed that, while "unknown," it was definitely the "bad" option for the afterlife.

Those who believe in heaven, according to the survey, identified one of two methods to get to heaven. Some said it was by "trusting Jesus Christ." Another group contended that the way to get to heaven was to lead "an exemplary life." Even some of those who identified themselves as either agnostic or atheist still expressed belief in heaven and hell and even believed that the way to get to heaven was the same as those with religious beliefs — trust in God or an exemplary life. It then seems reasonable to assume that people would want to avoid hell and therefore would do, or believe, what is necessary to get to heaven. We could expect that most people would live in such a way so as to avoid hell and achieve heaven. But if we observe Americans and American culture, do we see the majority of people living exemplary lives? Are they trusting Jesus and living according to His Gospel? We don't need a high-priced survey to find that answer. Violence, theft, cheating in business, lack of charity, lying, et cetera, are much easier to identify than exemplary lives.

Do the Statistics Lie?

If so many people believe in heaven and hell while also believing that this life will determine which destination will be theirs, why don't we see more evidence of that belief? The same survey asked the respondents where they expected to go upon death. Only one half of one percent responded that they thought hell was a real possibility for them! The vast majority believed they were destined for heaven. Ah, there is the rub! If I believe, given my present lifestyle, that I am destined for heaven, I have very little motivation to change my life. So, if there is a hell, it is meant for the other and not for me. If the responses on the survey are true, perhaps the worst thing about hell will be that it is a very lonely place because so few people reside or will reside there.

If we are all going to heaven, then the consideration of the last things is fairly meaningless other than as an esoteric discussion. Certainly if what I believe and how I live have nothing to do with my eternal destiny, then the most appropriate response may be, "The hell with it!" Belief and exemplary living are just a waste of time. And you should try to get a refund for the price of this book.

Of course a survey only tells us what people believe. Those beliefs can be far from reality. For beliefs to be meaningful, they need to be grounded in reality. And therein are the questions we must ask: "What is the reality? And how does it, or should it, affect the way I live now?" What can we learn from observing life from the perspective of Christian teaching? What do we see when we take the opportunity to peer into our hearts?

Catholics profess that, as God's creation, we bear the imprint of the Creator. If this is true, the belief in the last things, including death and the afterlife, should make some sense. Those beliefs should find resonance in us who are creatures made in the image of the Creator. If some union with the eternal "Him" is our destiny — is what we are made for — then when we encounter the truth it should be reasonable.

And, perhaps most importantly, if the eternal destiny is knowable and is the final goal of each and every life, it should impact the way we live here and now. If a student knows that she will have a test on Friday, she will do well to study today. If the gardener has been told by the weather forecaster that the first frost will strike tonight, he should pick his crop or cover the plants. If there is a possibility that I could get a flat tire because tires do sometimes go flat, I should carry a spare in the trunk of my car. The level of certainty in the above three examples varies. If the girl goes to school on Friday, she most likely will have a test. The weather prediction is not quite as much of a surety, but the weatherman is trustworthy and trained, so the gardener is wise to heed the forecast. I may or may not have a flat tire on my next trip, but the experience of thousands of drivers testify to the possibility — so, if I am wise, I'll be ready in case it does happen.

These examples all focus on things that are passing and of relatively little consequence in relationship to the totality of my life. But what of those things that can have *eternal* consequences? Whether I am reasonably sure (like the student), or fairly certain because of expert advice (like the gardener), or merely know that the testimony of others should make me consider the possibility (like the driver), the future should affect how I live today in preparation for what is to come.

Future events, especially final or last things, should make the reasonable person consider the consequences of today's events, his attitudes, and his ways of thinking and of acting. If it makes sense to study for the test, pick the crop, or carry a spare, then it also makes sense to live life in such a way that I obtain eternal life with God in heaven.

What we can know about these realities and how we integrate that knowledge into our lives is important. The philosopher and teacher Peter Kreeft speaks to the core of the matter: "In the light of death, everything takes on extreme value to us, and every choice takes on extreme and heroic importance."[5]

If he is wise, a "man lives with one eye on death"[6] because "the meaning of his death reveals the meaning of his life."[7]

So it is important to understand heaven and hell and everything else that can be learned about last things, for they have consequence in our present lives. Knowing the last things of this life will give us pointers on how to live it. And it is possible to know much about death and the life that follows it. As stated previously, we can obtain some truth from reflection on this life — what we see, feel, experience, and so forth. But still there is a veil between this world and the next. And so we must look both to experts and the testimony of others. This calls for faith that is reasoned. We should not have to take a blind leap to realize something that is so important — *eternally* important. Faith at its basis is a gift, but it is not blind. So we will examine what the Church teaches and what other witnesses have proclaimed. And what we consider, if it is true, should resonate truth in our hearts and minds. It should make sense (although not always perfect sense) to our intellect and to our spirit.

Faith must be able to stand strong before the questions about death. "Real answers are answers to real questions. If faith is a real answer, it must face that real question; it must stand face to face with death. When faith and death thus meet, it is death, not faith that is changed."[8]

The Christian faith is in and through Christ. At His death the veil of the temple was torn asunder. His death and subsequent resurrection opened the possibility of a far greater understanding of the last things and of how the life on this side of the grave must be lived.

So let us examine death and the issues that surround it in light of the God-man, Jesus, who reveals His Father's plan to us. Ask the Holy Spirit to guide you, for He "constantly perfects faith by his gifts so that revelation may be more and more understood."[9]

**One short sleep past, we wake eternally,
And Death shall be no more; Death, thou shalt die.**

From poem, "Death Be Not Proud,"
John Donne, 1572-1631

FOR PERSONAL CONSIDERATION

1. Consider some examples where knowing a future reality determines how you live in the now. How does that knowledge bring freedom?

2. Can we know ultimate reality? What is the relationship of faith and reason? (Read CCC 74-95.)

CHAPTER 2

Heaven and Hell

Where will I go when I die? This is a good question, although perhaps a mistaken one. Heaven and hell are states of being rather than places. Physical reality requires location and so the question of "where" is appropriate. If I am in Pittsburgh, I cannot be in New York. All corporeal beings, dogs, fish, or men, must be somewhere. Pure spirits, however, are not limited by place. My spirit or soul is tied to my body while I am alive. Each human person is made of both body and soul, and therefore, until death and at the final, called General, judgment,[10] has a particular locus.

The reality of the spirit is quite different. For example, Scripture tells us that Jesus is seated at the right hand of the Father (Heb 1:3). Yet we know that He is also really and truly present in the Eucharist. When I receive that heavenly food in Holy Communion at Mass, He is really and truly present in me. That is possible because "spirit" is not bound to one place at a time. Location does not limit the presence of God. Unlike my spirit, which is restricted to my unique body, the Holy Spirit can reside in me at the same time that he is also making you His temple, His residence.

Angels are pure spirits. Again, Scripture tells us that they always are before the throne of God. Yet in a number of passages Scripture tells us that an angel or angels made an appearance on earth. Angels were seen by the shepherds, told of the birth of Jesus, and sang His praise (Lk 2:8-14). Gabriel appeared to Mary (Lk 1:26-33). In the Old Testament an angel spoke to Abraham (Gen 22) and helped Tobit (Tob 5, 6, 8, 12). It is a pious tradition of the Church that angels are our guardians thus giving them an earthly connection and responsibility.

When I die, my soul will be separated from my body. My corporeal being will still be visible after death and will be buried at a specific location that can be visited. However, my spirit will no longer be tied to my body. My spirit still has a personal identity after death. It is still "me," but I am freed from the body that I called "me" for the years that I was alive and walking around in this physical world. So place is no longer a valid concept for me (my soul) after death. Since our experience is so tied to place, it is very difficult to speak of my being without reference to location. So, for the sake of understanding, we continue to use the concept of location.

As mentioned previously, Scripture tells us that Jesus is "seated at the right hand of the Father" (Col 3:1). But it is not that Jesus has a physical chair that is next to a throne on which sits the Father. Rather this Scripture expresses a relationship that the Father and the eternally begotten Son share.

Similarly, when Jesus tells us that "in my Father's house are many rooms" (Jn 14:2) and says, "I go to prepare a place for you" (Jn 14:2), this should not be taken as a literal house with a room with specific dimensions and a particular color to the walls. Rather, Jesus is giving us a physical analogy to help us understand a spiritual reality. The *Catechism of the Catholic Church* clarifies the reality: "This biblical expression does not mean a place ("space"), but a way of being" (CCC 2794).

Heaven is a spiritual homecoming. The person has completed his earthly pilgrimage and his soul, freed from the confines of a specific space, has come into the presence of God. In heaven we will be with God in a most intimate relationship — an intimacy that was not possible when we were tied to our bodies. Relationship is the essence of heaven. Again, the *Catechism of the Catholic Church* helps us with the concept: "To live in heaven is 'to be with Christ.' The elect live 'in Christ' (Phil

1:23; cf. Jn 14:3; 1 Thess 4:17), but they retain, or rather find, their true identity" (CCC 1025).

It is very difficult to speak of heaven without some physical analogy to help our minds comprehend the reality. However, sometimes the analogies produce more confusion than clarity. For example, it has often been said and sung that the streets of heaven are paved with gold. The response from the cynic is to say; "Streets of asphalt suit me fine, thank you!" Sometimes people will identify heaven with some favorite item or activity of earth. So the avid golfer is tempted to view heaven as a sort of Pebble Beach golf course where he or she will regularly break par. The dessert gourmet may think of heaven as the ongoing experience of eating the perfect cheesecake. These analogies may have a certain appeal, but eternal golf or the perfect cheesecake doesn't really offer eternal satisfaction.

What then is the identity of this last place, and why should someone desire it enough to let that desire influence the way he lives today?

The Heart's Search

Life is often a search for fulfillment. That quest may take the person down pathways that are self-destructive. Desires, such as sex, drugs, wealth, power, and so on, although providing a brief satisfaction, are ultimately empty. But there are also "good" and altruistic goals that only partially fulfill us. Dedication to and living for a spouse and family are wonderful motivations and often give a person a sense of satisfaction and fulfillment. This living for others does provide much satisfaction, but I have yet to meet the husband who is totally fulfilled by family alone. Even if the sense of fulfillment is great, children can disappoint, health problems can limit enjoyment, and, ultimately, death will bring parting. It is the same for other worthy endeavors: service to others, patriotism, artistic expression, et cetera.

No matter how wonderful the earthly experience, there remains a sense of imperfect happiness. Earthly experience, no matter how wonderful, will fall short — will fail to provide ultimate fulfillment.

Man was made for a relationship with God. The Garden of Eden (cf. Gen 2) provides a sense of man's fulfillment. There man's relationship with God was the source of all other goods that man experienced. God placed man in the garden, gave him authority, and supplied him with another that made two (man and woman) in a unity that was more than the sum of the individual parts. All of the various goods came from God and man's relationship to Him. Fulfillment was found not in the situations and gifts from God but in the *relationship* with God.

The sin of Adam and Eve resulted in expulsion from the Garden, a new struggle to live, a tendency to sin, and division within the family (see the story of Cain and Abel, Gen 4:1-16) — all of which we continue to experience.

Even though we are in a fallen state, we are still made in God's image. It is when we are most god-like that we taste a tiny amount of fulfillment. A job well done or holding a newborn child is an experience that gives us a deep joy. Also, it is in times like these that we most resemble our heavenly Father who created all and who is the Lord of life.

But the greatest loss that man has suffered is the loss of a close intimacy with God. This relationship with God, for which man was made, can no longer be experienced as it was in that first garden when the world was new. Men and women feel the pain of that loss, but not often are they able to name it. Needs are identified as hunger, thirst, hardship, loss of life, and so forth. These struggles are results of the fall and are now part of the human condition. The source of the struggles is found in the broken relationship with God. Mankind can seek solutions to the difficulties through science, medicine, and other efforts. But these efforts only aim at the result of the fall and not at the *cause* — the broken relationship with the Creator and Father. Solutions are sought in a variety of ways and places, when each soul is really longing for a deep intimate relationship with God as was available to Adam and Eve. Only God can quench the thirsty soul, only He can feed the spirit, and life eternal is found only through and in Him.

Heaven, then, is the fulfillment of the deepest desire of man. Heaven is the beatific vision — seeing God as He truly is, relating to Him as we were made to do. Heaven is the fulfillment of hope. In the heavenly relationship with God we find the answer to all of life's questions and longings. The lack and emptiness that plagued us even during the best times of our lives find answer and fulfillment in heaven. "Heaven is the ultimate end and fulfillment of the deepest human longings, the state of supreme definitive happiness" (CCC 1024).

If the streets are paved with gold, if chocolate grows on every bush, or if the best golf course awaits us, we won't notice because we will find in God what was intended for us from the beginning. Faith and hope will be unnecessary, for love will be fulfilled as God embraces us eternally. In the light of heaven, all other realities, even those in which we have found the deepest happiness on earth, will appear as nothing in the light of "the surpassing worth of knowing Christ Jesus" (Phil 3:8).

[We Christians] are persuaded that when we are removed from this present life we shall live another life, better than the present one.... Then we shall abide near God, changeless and free from suffering in the soul ... or if we fall with the rest, a worse one and in fire; for God has not made us as sheep or beasts of burden, a mere incidental work, that we should perish and be annihilated.

Athenagoras, *Plea on Behalf of the Christians*, 31

The joys we have on earth will pale in the light of glory. Our frame of reference will change. Now we see creation in light of

how it makes us happy or fulfilled. In heaven we will see everything through the spectrum of the answer to all questions, the
fulfillment of all desires, the light that dispels all darkness, the
reality that makes all else surreal. The often-repeated saying of
St. Augustine is true: "The soul is restless until it rests in God,"
and how wonderful if we find that for eternity.

What about Hell?

Heaven, then, is the fulfillment of our dreams, the filling of all
emptiness, the sweetness to which nothing else can compare. It
is hope realized. It is existence encompassed by Love. Hell is
the antithesis of heaven. It is shattered dreams, total emptiness,
bitterness far beyond any other that could be experienced. It is
hope unrealized. It is love denied and replaced with chains of
total selfishness and self hate.

Heaven cannot be earned. It is free gift of God. Jesus by His
life, death, and resurrection is the key that opens the gate — the
possibility of fulfillment and all that means. To open the door
we grasp the Key and treasure it above all else.

Hell is like heaven in only one sense. It too cannot be earned.
The redemption of Jesus is all-sufficient. Our worst sins are not
beyond God's power to forgive. His salvation is more than sufficient to keep hell empty for all eternity. Christ offers the key
— Himself — to all people. No one can say that they were
denied heaven because the work of Christ was insufficient. But
Scripture tells us that hell is not empty. Jesus lets us know as
much.[11] We cannot earn hell but we can freely choose it by reject-
ing the Key to heaven or, having once received it, choosing to
discard it. The *Catechism of the Catholic Church* states: "God pre-
destines no one to go to hell (cf. Council of Orange II [529]:
DS 397; Council of Trent [1547]: 1567); for this, a willful turn-
ing away from God (a mortal sin) is necessary, and persistence
in it until the end" (CCC 1037).

If we were able to say that we *earned* hell there might be
some satisfaction to be gained. But even that satisfaction will

be unavailable. The bitterness of hell will be the knowledge that a gift was squandered. At each person's particular judgment,[12] he who has rejected God will see the glory of the fulfillment that is only available in heaven. Having seen for what he was made, the reprobate will know eternal emptiness. He who has chosen hell will be plagued with an ongoing — eternal — lack of fulfillment. Damnation will be the ever-present knowledge that heaven could have been gained.

Scripture speaks of hell as fire that continues to burn but fails to consume (Ps 11:6; Mt 3:12, 13:42, 18:8-9; Lk 3:17). We have some idea of the effects of fire on flesh, but what is fire on the spirit? The disciples on the road to Emmaus saw and spoke to Jesus. They said: "Did not our hearts burn within us while he talked to us on the road?" (Lk 24:32). These two disciples were experiencing a new understanding of the word of God as explained by the Word of God, Christ. They were hungry for more. They had caught a glimpse of the Answer and they didn't want Him to leave; so they begged Him: "Stay with us." Jesus did, and the result was that their eyes were opened and they saw Him. They experienced great joy and communion. Their hearts burned while they were on the road, but His self-revelation and their union with Him through the Eucharist gave fulfillment to their burning desire for more.

The hearts of those in hell will also burn, but without any hope of the fire being quenched. They will know that their spirit longs for God, but they will know it is eternally unattainable. Hell is a constant burning without the slightest drop of hope to quench the eternal thirst.

The Here and Now

Knowing that heaven is our goal gives direction to our lives on earth. We will judge value by whether it draws us closer to God or drives us further away. Life is a continuing decision. Am I marching toward heaven or backing into hell?

When we pray the Act of Contrition, we say that we are sorry for our sins because of fear of hell and/or love of God. Love of God is the heart attitude for which we must always strive. Heaven will be the bridegroom (Christ) united with His bride (you and me). We are headed for a mystical marriage with our Lord — a marriage that shows the union of a husband and wife on earth to be a mere shadow of a far greater reality. Nonetheless, a healthy fear can also help us on our journey to our heavenly home. Many a youngster has avoided a sin because of love of his or her mother. Many others have avoided sin because of fear of their fathers. Both help the child to stay the right course.

Love of the God who offers us eternal happiness and fear of the alternative can and should make a difference in how we live today.

> **If we do the will of Christ, we shall obtain rest; but if not, if we neglect his commandments, nothing will rescue us from eternal punishment.**
>
> *Second Clement*, 5:5

FOR PERSONAL CONSIDERATION

1. When you pray the Our Father, you say, "Our Father, who art in heaven." What are you saying in this prayer? How is it a prayer? Read CCC 2794-2796 and consider the meaning of this line from the Our Father.

2. Name some other words or phrases in the Bible that are used to describe heaven. See CCC 1027.

3. Who will be in hell at the end of time? See CCC 1034.

CHAPTER 3

Purgatory

Nothing that is unclean can exist in the presence of the perfect God (cf. Rev 21:27). Most of us, when we examine ourselves honestly, will say that we are not ready to come into the presence of the all-holy God. Moses hid his face in the presence of God (Ex 3:6) and later hid in the cleft of a rock as God passed by (Ex 33:21). Elijah hid his face under his cloak when God was near (1 Kings 19:13). If these giants of the faith found themselves unworthy, then what of us? In fact, the normal reaction to the presence of God is to fall prostrate on the ground. God told Moses "man shall not see me and live" (Ex 33:20). If we are to see God, anything in or of us that is not in and of Christ must die. Those who would see God must be pure of heart (cf. Mt 5:8).

It is a basic tenet of our faith that we all need salvation and that we are saved by the gracious gift of God through Christ (CCC 389). We are also creatures with free will who can accept or reject God's gifts and graces. If we are seeking a home that is above (Col 3:1), we must continually yield to the God who calls us. We are to cooperate with His grace, to suffer with Him, and love the Church that he founded. We are to strive to grow in grace and to overcome faults. We must seek to make our lives an ongoing "yes" to the Holy Spirit — fostering an attitude that proclaims, "Lord 'send me' (Is 6:8) where I can be useful in Your divine plan." We are to strive to be humble servants of the loving God with the same response that Mary, our Mother, spoke when she heard God's will proclaimed by an angel: "Let it be to me according to your word" (Lk 1:38), and as Jesus spoke in the Garden of Gethsemane, "Father ... not my will, but thine, be done" (Lk 22:42).

But at the end of our earthly lives, we still will need to say with the Scriptures: "We are unworthy servants" (Lk 17:10). Even, perhaps especially, the greatest saints were intensely aware of their faults and sins — venial though they may be.[13] If we are found to be "in Christ" we are saved and our salvation assured. But most of us will yet need to be further purified. Hans Urs von Balthasar writes, "In the anteroom of heaven each of us will be purified until he has acquired the disposition of perfect poverty."[14]

That anteroom is called purgatory. It is not so much a place as a process. Here the dross is burned away so that only pure gold remains. Von Balthasar describes it as acquiring "perfect poverty." When our hands are full, they can receive nothing else. Heaven and the beatific vision and all that accompanies that — things that are beyond our imagination — can only be placed into empty hands. Thus another way to view purgatory is that it is the opportunity to release everything, to which we cling so tightly, that is not God.

So, there then is a giving up — a letting go. But this is never a losing proposition. Man is made for God. We find fulfillment only when we are in the strong embrace of the Father. It is there that we find the answers to the deepest questions of the heart. Jesus gives us many parables to illustrate the unsurpassed value of embracing the living God and His truth. Recall the parable of the pearl of great price (Mt 13:45). The pearl merchant sells all that he has, probably including many other precious pearls, but he does it willingly. And when he obtains the pearl of great price, he doesn't bemoan the loss of the other pearls. Instead, he rejoices exceedingly in that one pearl that can compare to no other. Thus his "loss" is gain!

That which must drop from our hands, what must be burned off, what must be purified, is the work of purgatory. It is a merciful process. To stand in the presence of God in an unpurified state would be too much to endure. It is mercy to be rid of that which burdens us, so that we may be welcomed as forgiven sons and daughters into the mansion that has been prepared for us.

Frank Sheed, a great apologist and evangelist, said; "I can't conceive a future life without a possibility of cleansing (which is what the word purgatory means) not because I deserve it, but because I need it. The thought of entering the presence of the all-pure God as the spotted object that I am revolts me."[15]

In the scriptural picture of both purgatory and hell, fire is used as an image. However, there is a great difference between these two "fires." The fire of hell will eternally sear the soul that has freely chosen to reject her Savior. The twentieth chapter of Revelation shows that hell is for the unsaved. "If any one's name was not found written in the book of life, he was thrown into the lake of fire" (Rev 20:15).

The fire of purgatory is of a different nature. One Scripture that is often tied to an understanding of purgatory is 1 Corinthians 3:15; "If any man's work is burned up, he will suffer loss, though he himself will be saved, but only as through fire." Again this Scripture seems to point to the effect of the "fire" of purgatory as dealing with the "straw" in a person's life (see 1 Cor 3:12 and the parable of the wheat and tares in Mt 13:25-30). St. Augustine reflecting on this verse wrote, "Some will be saved through a purifying fire; for a long or short period depending on the extent to which they were attached to things which do not endure."[16]

Duration

St. Augustine speaks of the duration of purgatory as "a long or short period." Again, we find it necessary to speak in temporal terms to better understand what occurs outside of time. But, rather than time, there is a difference in degree of required purification. The extent of purification is dependent upon the state of the soul that is being purified. Some will require more purification than others. It is also true that prayers and sacrifices offered for the souls undergoing purification can be effective in hastening the process. This will be discussed further in Chapter 5, "Prayer for the Deceased."

Purgatory is also a passing state of being. Heaven and hell are eternal, but purgatory will only last until the second coming of Jesus at the end of time. Then there will be a final judgment and all will be assigned to their eternal destiny. Purgatory will no longer be necessary. The saved, who have been fully cleansed, will have no more need of the transition of purgatory.

FOR PERSONAL CONSIDERATION

1. Read Hebrews 12:7-11. Why is the cleansing of purgatory a blessing? Consider this quote: "For [St. Catherine of Genoa], purgatory is a gift of God's mercy permitting us to cooperate with his grace in removing all the obstacles that we put between ourselves and his love."[17]

2. Read CCC 1030-1031. What faults can be dealt with in purgatory?

3. Read the quotes below. What do they add to your understanding of purgatory?

> **Purgatory ... is always a matter of one thing: the painful, unavoidable experience of being confessed by God, the removal of all hidden egoism until the moment when the soul is no longer preoccupied with its own individual salvation and existence, but only with one thing: that God has been offended by the sins of this world ... and the soul would be ready to persevere in bearing pain for as long as necessary to atone for the guilt of the world: here it has entered into his disposition and is taken up into heaven.**
>
> Hans Urs von Balthasar, *First Glance at Adrienne von Speyr*
> Translated by Antje Lawry and Sr. Sergia Englund, O.C.D
> (San Francisco: Ignatius Press, 1981), p. 56

> **Purgatory is for those who are not quite "dead" enough, for those who have not yet wholly died to themselves. Since most people die with attachments to sin and self, they need further purification.**
>
> Ann Ball, *Catholic Book of the Dead*
> (Huntington, IN: Our Sunday Visitor, 1995), p. 23

CHAPTER 4

The Family of God

I hope you are making plans for the family reunion. The date has already been set. It will occur on the day of the Final Judgment. Those who have rejected the salvation offered to them by Christ through His suffering, death, and resurrection will be cast into the "lake of fire" (Rev 20:14). Those who are found "in Christ" (cf. Phil 3:9) will be called into the place that has been prepared for them in the "new heavens and a new earth" (2 Pet 3:13).

It will be quite a reunion of the family of God — all the saints, those who have "washed their robes and made them white in the blood of the Lamb" (Rev 7:14), will be there. It will be the social event to outdo all social events and it will last an eternity. It is a party that you won't want to miss.

But we don't need to wait until that final day to participate in that family of saints. If we are baptized and free of mortal sin, we are, right now, active members of that living family of God. That family goes by many names. The two most common names are the Body of Christ and the Communion of Saints.

The image of God's people as a body appears in several places in Scripture.[18] Christ is the head of that body and we are the members. The same concept is evident in the image of the vine (Jesus) and the branches (all of us).[19] In both images the foundational concept is that we have life because we are connected to the head or to the vine. In other words, life comes through our connection with Jesus.

But there arises one other question. Who are "those" who are united to Christ? The answer lies in understanding the concept of the "Body of Christ." Jesus, like any being, has only one body.

His disciples are the members of His body. Christ's followers can be found in heaven, in purgatory, and on the earth. Therefore, the heavenly, purgatorial, and earthly believers are those who are in the body of Christ. And because these believers are all united to Christ, they are also united with each other.

Saints are those who have been made holy and therein have been saved. We certainly call the inhabitants of heaven saints. Some of these saints are canonized, and we celebrate their lives and strive to follow their example. But there are others in heaven whose names we do not know. Even these unnamed saints are celebrated in the Church's liturgical year on the feast of All Saints (November 1).

But the concept of "saint" goes beyond the residents of heaven. Remember that "saint" refers to someone made "holy" and "worthy" in and through Christ and, therefore, are saved from the fires of hell and destined for the eternal kingdom of God. Thus those who are undergoing the purification of purgatory are also saints. They have not reached their crown of "sainthood" in heaven but they are saved. For the members of Christ's body who are in purgatory, there is only one direction and that is up to heaven. No one in purgatory will end up in hell. Purgatory is populated by the saved — those who have been made worthy by the cross of Christ. Yes, they still need some scrubbing to be pure enough to stand in the heavenly court, but there is no doubt that they are "saints."

Traditionally, the faithful in purgatory are called the Church Suffering, while the saved in heaven are called the Church Triumphant. The state of being of these two groups is different. Some are triumphant and some are suffering, but all are members of the Church — members of the Body of Christ and branches on the true Vine.

And there is another group that needs to be considered. Collectively these individuals are known as the Church Militant. These are the "saints" that are here on earth, the baptized who are living in the state of grace — hopefully all of the readers (and hopefully the writer!) of this book. And if some reader is not in this category because he or she has not accepted the gracious gift of God and been baptized, or because he or she is burdened by a mortal sin, then that person remains *potentially* a saint. Christ offers salvation to all of us living and breathing mortals; He invites all of us to become members of the one Body. The Vine has sufficient room for more branches to be engrafted. We are, or can be, made worthy and holy. We are all saints or potential saints.

Now there is one very significant difference between the Church Militant and the combined Church Triumphant and Suffering. Our fate is not yet sealed. We can opt out of the Body. We can be torn from the Vine by choosing sin and self instead of Savior and Lord. We can disregard the invitation and miss that family reunion at the end of time.

Indeed Christ has one Body that is manifest in heaven, on earth, and in purgatory. And in this we come to understand another term used to describe God's family — the Communion of Saints. Communion is "the act of sharing; . . . participation." It is "an intimate relationship."[20] We share life with all the other saints. We can ask them to pray for us and we can pray for others who share this intimacy of union in Christ.[21]

The Communion of Saints is a "Last Thing" because it is a lasting thing. It is worth cultivating love for the saints in all three states of existence because we will be spending eternity with them. We may disagree with other members of the Body of Christ. We may prefer the company of some certain individuals rather than some others. We may dislike the personality of some other earthly saint — perhaps someone in your parish or even in your natural family. We may find some individual saints to be downright annoying. But we must never forget that we are brothers and sisters who, by God's mercy and through continued yielding to Him, will share eternity together. We do not choose our family members. They become our brothers and sisters because they are called by Christ and enter freely into the family through

His grace. God loves all His children. Christ put a high premium on the unity of His Church at the Last Supper when He prayed that we all would be united (Jn 17:20). We, His children — His saints — living in this particular time period in earthly history, must pray and work for unity. We must make love of the earthly saints and love of potential saints (i.e., all those who are living and breathing right now but separated from the body of Christ) one of our highest priorities.

Don't Forget Our Mother

One of the heavenly and canonized saints deserves our special attention. As we have already indicated, all of the saints are our brothers and sisters. Even Jesus is identified as the "first-born among many brethren" (Rom 8:29). But one of our sisters in heaven is also our Mother. Mary said yes to an angel who was sent to her by God with the most earth (and heaven) shaking request of all history — nay, of all eternity. Mary was asked to be the Mother of God. When she said yes, the Second Person of the Trinity took on flesh in her virginal womb. By her yes and by "the power of the Most High" (Lk 1:35) she became the Mother of Jesus, true God and true man.

If Jesus is our elder brother, then Mary is our Mother as well. In fact, Pope St. Pius X writes that since we are all members of the body of Christ and in light of the fact that the physical body of Christ spent nine months in the womb of Mary, we "in a spiritual and mystical sense are ... the children of Mary and she is the Mother of us all."[22]

Because of this the Catholic Church has paid special honor to Mary. As our Mother, through whom life came to us,[23] she is always worthy of greater honor than any other creature — an honor that the Church calls *hyperdulia*.[24] We are encouraged to often seek her intercession because of the special love she has for us as her dear children.

> **Spoken by a French country priest to a woman distraught by death:**
>
> **"But at least I can assure you of this: there are not two separate kingdoms, one for the living, and one for the dead. There is only God's Kingdom and, living or dead, we are all therein."**
>
> George Bernanos, *The Diary of a Country Priest*
> Translated from the French by Pamela Morris
> (Carroll & Graf: New York, 1983), p. 170

FOR PERSONAL CONSIDERATION

1. Is there someone who particularly annoys you? Is there someone whom you find difficult to love? Is there division in your family? Write those names on a piece of paper and carry it with you. Regularly look at those names and pray for those individuals asking God to help you love them, because they are His children and your brothers and/or sisters.

2. How is your relationship with your heavenly Mother, Mary? Read CCC 967-969. Talk to Mary about your concerns and ask for her intercession.

3. The concept of the Communion of Saints has very practical implications for your life. Read CCC 954-959. How can you strengthen your relationship with other members of Christ's family?

CHAPTER 5

Prayer for the Deceased

Love is stronger than death. It is not negated by the grave. There are few things sadder than watching someone who lacks faith standing at the casket of a loved one. The phrase, "He *lost* a loved one to death" is commonly heard. The person's grief is totally centered on the "loss" that occurs because of death.

We, as Catholics, grieve at the death of someone close to us. Physical intimacy with the departed person is gone. The comfort of a hug or a kiss is sorely missed. The conversations over coffee or tea will no longer give us the solace that they did before. Yes we *feel* a loss, but in truth that person, that loved one, is *not* lost to us.

As we discussed in the previous chapter, we on earth remain united with those in heaven and in purgatory in the Communion of Saints. Love binds us together in the Body of Christ. Even though we may no longer see, hear, or physically touch the person who has died, we remain connected. Love does transcend the grave.

"Life is not ended; it is merely changed."[25] The deceased has "put aside his mortal frame and put on immortality."[26] We do not know the exact status of the deceased. That person may have been taken directly to heaven. She may be undergoing purification. He, God forbid, may be experiencing the utter despair of eternal death in hell.

There is a very interesting story in the Scripture about a beggar named Lazarus and a wealthy man (Lk 16:19-31). Both the pauper and the wealthy man died on the same day. The beggar went to his reward and was held in the bosom of Abraham (v. 23) while the wealthy man was burning in fiery Hades. The wealthy man, who in the afterlife is now extremely poor, destitute, and confined to an eternity of horror, asks two things. First he requests a little water be brought by Lazarus to quench his unending thirst. This is denied him — those in hell are beyond the reach of the saved. He then asks that Lazarus be sent to those people that the wealthy man had loved on earth. This wish is also not granted for those on earth have the Scriptures and the witness of Jesus from which to learn (v. 31). This story is to teach and encourage us.

If the deceased, whom we have loved, could send a message to us it would be to live in such a way that at the end of this life we would recline in the embrace of Abraham, our father in faith, rather than be confined to the fiery furnace of hell. On the eternal side of the grave, perspective is gained and sight sharpened. In this life we do not see reality in its fullness. "Now we see in a mirror dimly, but then face to face" (1 Cor 13:12a). Those who have died have seen reality clearly and they, as the wealthy man and as Lazarus, would want us to know that we should embrace the life of Jesus and live fully in his grace.

So the deceased want us to hear the message that is already available to us in the Scriptures. But can we do anything for those who have died? Can our love effectively reach beyond the grave? The answer is yes and no. As the wealthy man could do nothing for his relatives and friends on earth, we can do nothing for those in hell — their fate is sealed. Those in heaven, although we remain united to them in the Body of Christ, are perfectly happy and need nothing else. They can, however, pray for us and we can ask them to do so. It is the Church suffering, those in purgatory, for whom we can do an effective work of love. Since they remain connected to us, we can express effective love for them.

Love Made Us for Love

Quite often we experience life in a way that confirms the reality of God and His truth. For example, we all experience a deep internal longing, and we strive to fill that hole in our lives. As Catholics we understand that only God can fill it. When we accept that truth, we experience a certain inner peace even while looking forward to its fulfillment in heaven.

Similarly there are situations in our lives against which we rebel. For example, only the insane or the totally depraved would argue against the value of goodness and justice. Made in God's image, we innately praise these virtues. There is also something in our make-up that rebels against the thought that death can separate us from those whom we love.

Have you ever observed a person standing at the foot of the grave of a departed spouse and talking with the "departed" person? It happens all the time. Why? The answer lies partly in the fact that our innermost being rebels against the thought that love, something that is a bedrock experience in our life, is ended by death. If death is truly the end of the one we love, then nothing makes sense. We are but tragic figures in a black drama of immense despair and gloom.

But God made us in His image. Even though we are damaged by sin and concupiscence,[27] even though our life compass doesn't always point true, we still hold the breath of God. When our spirit rebels against the separation brought on by death, it is identifying something that is eternally true. We leave this life, but only to enter into eternal life. In death much of what we know as normal life will pass out of existence, but love does not fail. Love is of the very essence of eternity, for God in the Trinity is perfect love and real life in the truest sense. And He shares that with us who are united to Him.

What practically can we do for the departed? We can pray. We pray knowing that God hears our prayers (CCC 2616). We pray knowing that prayer makes a difference. We pray because prayer brings us in touch with the eternal, where he or she whom we love has gone. We pray because Christ has taught us to pray and has shown us how by his example. Did Christ not respond to the "prayer" of Mary and Martha for their brother,

Lazarus, who had died? Did not Lazarus experience the effects of that prayer? We can pray for the departed relying on the grace of Jesus and the power of the Holy Spirit.

The wealthy man in the gospel story could receive no water to quench his thirst. Our prayers can do nothing for those in hell. But our prayers can "quench the thirst" of those in purgatory. God allows our prayers and sacrifices to hasten their purification. Love is always life giving and our love offered in prayer for someone in purgatory pleases God and is effective. And the greatest prayer of love, the Eucharistic sacrifice of Christ, can be offered for the deceased.

The *Catechism of the Catholic Church* provides a list of ways to love those in purgatory: "From the beginning the church has honored the memory of the dead and offered prayers in suffrage for them, above all the Eucharistic sacrifice, so that, thus purified, they may attain the beatific vision of God (cf. Council of Lions II [1274]: DS 856). The Church also commends almsgiving, indulgences, and works of penance undertaken on behalf of the dead" (CCC 1032).

The Church has always exhorted us to pray for the dead. She invites believers to look upon the mystery of death not as the last word on human fate, but as the passage toward eternal life.... It is important and proper to pray for the dead because, even if they died in grace and in friendship with God, perhaps they still have need of a further purification to enter into the joy of heaven.

Address by Pope John Paul II
Angelus, All Souls Day, November 2, 2003

> They whom we love and lose are no longer where they were before. They are now wherever we are.
>
> St. John Chrysostom

FOR PERSONAL CONSIDERATION

1. Call to mind your loved ones, friends, or relatives who have died. Offer prayers and small sacrifices for them today.

2. Offer a prayer for those in purgatory who have no one to pray for them, perhaps using the prayer in the appendix of this book.

3. Visit the cemetery where your family members are buried. Read and contemplate Psalm 146.

CHAPTER 6

Resurrection of the Body

You and I are unique in the universe. We are not mere animals. We do share similar flesh, blood, bone, molecules, atoms, and subatomic parts with the beasts, but we stand above them because we have a uniqueness that they lack. We have an eternal soul that makes us persons and differentiates us from the beast. But at the same time we are not angels. They are spirit as are we, but they lack flesh, bone, et cetera. Shylock in Shakespeare's *Merchant of Venice* identifies some of what we humans share: "If you prick us, do we not bleed? If you tickle us, do we not laugh? If you poison us, do we not die?" (Act 3, Scene 1). There is no bleeding, tickling, or poisoning of pure spirits.

We are then a unique blend of physical and spirit, and it is a combination that has existed from the very beginning. Adam and Eve could leave footprints when they walked in the Garden of Eden. If they touched an animal in the Garden, the animal felt it. Yet our first parents, made in God's image, were spiritual beings as well. As a consequence of their higher state of existence, man was given authority over the animals (cf. Gen 1:26).

We are well aware of the course of the story of Genesis. Man (female and male) sinned and suffered the consequences. And because Adam and Eve were both physical and spiritual, both aspects of their lives were affected. They suffered pain and they had to work hard to eke out a living. They would experience death as an evil. The two (man and woman), who had been one, now found that there was a wedge in their relationship. Their minds were darkened to aspects of the truth. Even as they tried to live godly lives, they found that temptation and sin still plagued them (cf. Rom 7:21-23).

Man could not extricate himself from this disastrous situation. Sin had created a gap so wide between man and God that man could not bridge it. But God in His mercy had a plan and gave a promise (Gen 3:15). In "the fulness of time" (Eph 1:10), Jesus, the Second Person of the Triune God, took flesh and became man. His suffering, death, and resurrection bridged the gap. The God-man expiated the sin of man and invited us through Him to come to the Father.

Everyone who had been born from the beginning of time up to the minute that Jesus placed Himself into His Father's hands and died on the cross, if he or she trusted in God, was given salvation through Christ. Time was no barrier to the salvation of Christ. Thus, all who lived before the incarnation of Christ were saved only through Him. And those who have been born after Calvary enter into a saving relationship with God through Baptism.[28] When a person dies with Christ in Baptism, he is raised to life with Him (Rom 6:4). If that person continues to respond to God's grace in obedience during his life, he will enjoy the beatific vision in the next.

So God has restored what man lost through the sin in the Garden of Eden. But has the restoration been fully completed? After all, in the garden man physically related to God. Since man's nature is body and soul, God's plan for man included an idyllic life to be enjoyed as a full human being — flesh, blood, and soul. Now when we die our physical body decays, while our spiritual being is judged and invited into heaven or cast into hell. Is it then only our souls that are saved? Is God's salvation incomplete?

In the Apostles' Creed we proclaim that we believe in "the resurrection of the body, and the life everlasting." We are saved and we are being saved. Jesus' death and resurrection reached back through history to give salvation to those before His time. It also reaches forward for the establishment of "a new heaven and a new earth" (Rev 21:1).

At the end of time, God's original intent for man will again be fully evident. We will dwell in the kingdom of God as both corporeal and spiritual beings. If God's original plan is not to be fully reestablished, then our sin will have proved to be stronger than God's redemption. And that is an utter impossibility. Jesus is fully triumphant over evil, and the fullness of His victory will become apparent when the graves are opened and each and every soul and body are reunited. "For the Lord himself will descend from heaven with a cry of command, with the archangel's call, and with the sound of the trumpet of God. And the dead in Christ will rise" (1 Thess 4:16). The saved will then dwell in the eternal kingdom of God.

But how can we be so sure of this promised life? Well, there are many signs that point toward the reality. First, the resurrected body of Jesus is in heaven. Jesus is still God-*man*. The apostles and many others saw His resurrected body. Forty days after his resurrection, Jesus ascended to his Father. The disciples saw Him physically leave. And an angel told them that just as He had left so He would return.

The nature and the substance of the resurrected Jesus are interesting. Thomas, who initially doubted the resurrection, could touch the body of Jesus (Jn 20:27); yet Jesus could pass through locked doors (Jn 20:19). At times the disciples had difficulty in recognizing Jesus. Mary Magdalene thought He was a gardener (Jn 20:15). While on the road to Emmaus, two disciples walked and talked with Him and yet did not recognize him until the breaking of the bread (Lk 24:13-35). Yet in each instance these individuals knew that they were talking to a real man and not some ghost.

In each instance, He was always and unmistakably recognizable as Jesus. When He met some of the apostles who were fishing, initially they did not recognize Him. But when they caught a large haul of fish at Jesus' command, Peter exclaimed, "It is the Lord!" (Jn 21:7). Jesus was even cooking some food for them — an activity that demands physical hands. When Jesus first appeared to the disciples in the upper room (Jn 20:19-23), they knew that it was Jesus. Jesus even "breathed on them."

So this resurrected body is truly Jesus, and it is physical. Yet the physicality is not like anything that we experience now. It is a glorified body. And we know from the Scriptures that this is a promise for us as well. As St. Paul writes, "The trumpet will sound, and the dead will be raised imperishable, and we shall be changed. For this perishable nature must put on the imperishable, and this mortal nature must put on immortality" (1 Cor 15:52-53).

But Jesus is not the only body in heaven. The Assumption is a defined dogma of the Catholic Faith. Mary was taken to heaven both body and soul. As hard as you may seek, you cannot find the grave of Mary, the mother of Jesus, because at her passing there was no body to bury. It was assumed into heaven — another foretaste of what will happen to all at the end of the world. The *Catechism of the Catholic Church* states: "The Assumption of the Blessed Virgin is a singular participation in her Son's Resurrection and an anticipation of the resurrection of other Christians" (CCC 966). Note especially that Mary's Assumption is a direct result of her only Son's life, death, and resurrection. Our hope has the same foundation.

There is one other interesting hint of a transformed body that is given to us in Scripture. "Jesus took with him Peter and James and John his brother, and led them up a high mountain apart. And he was transfigured before them, and his face shone like the sun, and his garments became white as light. And behold, there appeared to them Moses and Elijah, talking with him" (Mt 17:1-3). The body of Jesus became different. It was Jesus standing on that hill, but in a way that the three disciples could plainly see was different. Then two others joined Jesus: Moses and Elijah. These two individuals represented the Old Covenant. Moses was the lawgiver, while Elijah embodied the prophetic tradition. In the Old Covenant and in Jewish tradition, the departure of Moses and Elijah did not happen in a normal manner. We read that Elijah was taken to heaven in a fiery chariot (2 Kings 2:1-9). Meanwhile, before the Israelites entered into the Promised Land, Moses went up a mountain and was seen no more (Deut 34:1-9). Was that why they appeared in a physical manifestation with Jesus? Certainly Peter recognized them as three physical beings, for he volunteered to set up tents for them.

While the Resurrection, Ascension, and Assumption are defined dogmas, these thoughts about Moses and Elijah are only musings and conjecture. Perhaps some day when you, with your resurrected body, are walking with them in the garden of the fully established kingdom of God, you may want to put your hands on their shoulders and ask them personally.

Christ has been raised from the dead, the first fruits of those who have fallen asleep. For as by a man came death, by a man has come also the resurrection of the dead. For as in Adam all die, so also in Christ shall all be made alive. But each in his own order: Christ the first fruits, then at his coming those who belong to Christ. Then comes the end, when he delivers the kingdom to God the Father.

I Cor 15:20-24

After the resurrection, each person will have the same body (except for imperfections) that he had in this life. If this involves having the same matter, this is surely within God's power. No matter what happens to the body after death, He can recall and rebuild the material of the body.

Rev. William G. Most, "The Resurrection of the Body"
From *In Season, Out of Season: Meditations on the Sunday Gospels and Second Readings*

FOR PERSONAL CONSIDERATION

1. Read 1 Corinthians 15. What does Paul tell us about the resurrection of the dead?

2. Read CCC 999-1000. How is the Eucharist a foretaste of our own resurrection?

CHAPTER 7

The General Judgment

At death each person will be judged. Those who are found to be in Christ will be saved and proceed to heaven or to purgatory for a period of purification. Those who have chosen self, rejected Christ, and died in mortal sin, will be sent to the place assigned for them — hell.

Yet Scripture and the teaching of the Church also speak of another judgment — a final General Judgment. In the Nicene Creed we proclaim: "He [Jesus] will come again in glory to judge the living and the dead, and his kingdom will have no end." At the end of this world, when the kingdom of God is fully established, there will be a judgment of all men of history — those who had previously died and those who may be living on the last day of this present world.

When Jesus ascended to His Father, two angels informed those who were present that Jesus would return. "While they (the disciples) were gazing into heaven as he (Jesus) went, behold, two men stood by them in white robes, and said, 'Men of Galilee, why do you stand looking into heaven? This Jesus, who was taken up from you into heaven, will come in the same way as you saw him go into heaven'" (Acts 1:10-11).

There is much speculation about when Jesus will return, what signs will predict his second coming, and exactly who will be saved. Books are sold by the thousands that purport to know the scenario for the last times. This is not a new phenomenon. Such speculation has been around since the beginning of Christianity.

And there are many Scriptures that discuss the end times and what will precede the Second Coming of Jesus. Most of the twenty-fourth chapter of the Gospel of Matthew is a description of the end times. Among other prophesies, Jesus tells His disciples that "nation will rise against nation, and kingdom against kingdom, and there will be famines and earthquakes in various places: all this is but the beginning of the sufferings. . . . And many false prophets will arise and lead many astray. And because wickedness is multiplied, most men's love will grow cold. . . . [T]he sun will be darkened, and the moon will not give its light, and the stars will fall from heaven, and the powers of the heavens will be shaken" (Mt 24:7-8, 11-12, 29). And this is just one of many passages that describe the events surrounding the end of the world.[29]

The many Scriptures on the end times and the Second Coming of Jesus are worthy of reflection from both a global and a personal perspective. However, end times Scriptures need to be kept within the context of the entire Bible and the Tradition of the Church. The verses from Acts that are cited earlier are most illuminating. The angel asks the disciples, "Why do you stand looking into heaven?" Yes, the angel was telling them, Jesus will come again, but the disciples were not to spend their time "looking into heaven." Rather, they were to be about the work that Jesus had entrusted to them.

Christ's last instruction to his followers was: "Go therefore and make disciples of all nations, baptizing them in the name of the Father and of the Son and of the Holy Spirit, teaching them to observe all that I have commanded you; and lo, I am with you always, to the close of the age" (Mt 28:19-20). And this is exactly what they did. "They went forth and preached everywhere, while the Lord worked with them and confirmed the message by the signs that attended it" (Mk 16:20). And this continues to be the marching order for Christ's disciples. We are to expect His return because His promises are always true. And we are to ready ourselves for that final reckoning. However, too much "looking into heaven" can be contrary to our marching orders to go and preach the Good News!

The twenty-fifth chapter of Matthew gives us another very interesting insight into the Second Coming of Jesus and the General Judgment — a description that connects both the final judgment and God's expectation of us in this life. All mankind will be divided into two camps — the sheep and the goats. The sheep will comprise those who have done good to the least of the brethren (Mt 25:40). Those designated as goats will be those who did not do good to Christ's brethren (Mt 25:45). The sheep destined for life with God will receive the reward for their love and obedience. Meanwhile, the goats "will go away into eternal punishment" (Mt 25:46).

Why the Need for a General Judgment?

If we are judged at the time of our death, why is there the need for another, final judgment? Well, there are some loose ends to be tied up. There will be an end to this world as we know it and those on earth will need to be judged and their final condition established, while those in purgatory, which will cease to exist, need to finish their process of purification.

Additionally, the *Catechism of the Catholic Church* states that everything hidden will be revealed at this last judgment. "We shall know the ultimate meaning of the whole work of creation and of the entire economy of salvation and understand the marvellous ways by which his Providence led everything toward its final end. The Last Judgment will reveal that God's justice triumphs over all the injustice by his creatures and that God's love is stronger than death" (cf. Song 8:6) (CCC 1040).

Everyone's eyes will be opened. There will be no room for gainsayers because the fullness of truth will be evident to all — men, angels, and demons.

In addition, the Catholic faith is communal and the final judgment will emphasize the unity of God's people. Those judged righteous at the end of time will represent the full number of the Communion of Saints and of the Body of Christ. The followers of Jesus, the people of God, the Church everlasting, will be numbered and fully revealed. All will see the full manifestation of God's justice, mercy, and wisdom. The Last Judgment will occasion the Great Amen for which the world has waited since creation. With the entire glorious plan of God laid open to all, heaven will resound with the chorus: "Great and wonderful are thy deeds, O Lord God the Almighty!" (Rev 15:3b).

And being present at His judicial decision, all, both men and angels and demons, shall utter one voice saying, "Righteous is Your judgment" (Ps 118:137). Of which voice the justification will be seen in the awarding to each that which is just; since to those who have done well shall be assigned righteous eternal bliss, and to the lovers of iniquity shall be given eternal punishment. And the fire which is unquenchable and without end awaits these latter.

St. Hippolytus, *Refutation of All Heresies, 3*

FOR PERSONAL CONSIDERATION

1. Read Matthew 25:31-46. How are you reflecting the life of the sheep? The life of the goats? Ask the Holy Spirit to guide you to live the life that Christ expects. Commit to one area (feeding the hungry, comforting the sick, et cetera) where you can respond in a practical way during the coming week.

2. Read some of the Scriptures on the end times (Mt 10:12-24; 16:27; 24; Mk 13; Lk 21; and most of Revelation). Finish by praying an Our Father with particular attention to the petition "Thy kingdom come."

CHAPTER 8

New Heavens and a New Earth

As discussed in Chapter 6 on the resurrection of the body, man is made of both body and soul. That was man's initial condition at the creation of Adam and Eve; but, for each of us, it is temporarily disrupted at death when soul and body are separated. However, at the full revelation of Christ's victory at the end of time, the body and soul of each man and woman will be reunited. Where will the saved then live? God has revealed a marvelous plan.

The original Garden of Eden, where our first parents dwelt, was lost because of sin. Man was banished to a world quite different from the idyllic garden. God reveals to Adam and Eve the effect of their sin on the new land on which they shall dwell: "Cursed is the ground because of you; in toil you shall eat of it all the days of your life; thorns and thistles it shall bring forth to you; and you shall eat the plants of the field. In the sweat of your face you shall eat bread till you return to the ground, for out of it you were taken; you are dust, and to dust you shall return" (Gen 3:17-19). Quite a change from the garden where man had walked with God (cf. Gen 2:8)! But in the fullness of time the saved will have a new paradise to inhabit. There will be "new heavens and a new earth in which righteousness dwells" (2 Pet 3:13).

We long for that final coming when Christ's victory will be fully manifest. And we are not alone in that yearning. The Scriptures tell us, "the whole creation has been groaning in travail together until now" (Rom 8:22). Sin has brought disorder not only to humans but also to all creation. Man was given authority over the garden and over all of the plants and animals (cf. Gen 1:28-

30). When man fell into sin, all creation suffered from that fall. Efforts to preserve the environment or save the whales are worthy tasks, but our best ecological hopes and plans will fall short. As we cannot save ourselves, so creation cannot be "saved" and restored to God's original order until God's kingdom is fully established.

The book of Revelation provides the reader with a glimpse of the end times. John reveals the judgment that comes on the cusp of eternity, but he also provides a glimpse of the glory that awaits the children of God. He writes:

> Then I saw a new heaven and a new earth; for the first heaven and the first earth had passed away, and the sea was no more. And I saw the holy city, new Jerusalem, coming down out of heaven from God, prepared as a bride adorned for her husband; and I heard a loud voice from the throne saying, "Behold, the dwelling of God is with men. He will dwell with them, and they shall be his people, and God himself will be with them; he will wipe away every tear from their eyes, and death shall be no more, neither shall there be mourning nor crying nor pain any more, for the former things have passed away.
>
> And he who sat upon the throne said, "Behold, I make all things new."
>
> Rev 21:1-5

In the new garden of Paradise all men will dwell in unity and bask in a new Light. Scripture states that this new world will not need the sun or any other celestial body to provide light and heat for "night shall be no more; they need no light of lamp or sun, for the Lord God will be their light, and they shall reign for ever and ever" (Rev 22:5).

This new habitation for the redeemed is the "holy city" where Christ the Bridegroom will dwell with His bride (cf. Rev 22). The inhabitants here will enjoy "the beatific vision, in which God opens himself in an inexhaustible way to the elect." There will be an "ever-flowing well-spring of happiness, peace, and mutual communion" (CCC 1045).

Our language is at a loss to describe the wonders of the final blossoming of the kingdom of God. John in the book of Revelation can only use figurative language to hint at the glory and the majesty of the eternal home of the saints: "The foundations of the wall of the city were adorned with every jewel; the first was jasper, the second sapphire, the third agate, the fourth emerald, the fifth onyx, the sixth carnelian, the seventh chrysolite, the eighth beryl, the ninth topaz, the tenth chrysoprase, the eleventh jacinth, the twelfth amethyst. And the twelve gates were twelve pearls, each of the gates made of a single pearl, and the street of the city was pure gold, transparent as glass" (Rev 21:19-21).

It will be a place full of life, with "the river of the water of life, bright as crystal, flowing from the throne of God and of the Lamb through the middle of the street of the city; also, on either side of the river, the tree of life with its twelve kinds of fruit, yielding its fruit each month; and the leaves of the tree were for the healing of the nations. There shall no more be anything accursed, but the throne of God and of the Lamb shall be in it" (Rev 22:1-3).

As the old hymn proclaims, let's plan to meet on the glorious shores of that eternal kingdom:

> *Yes, we'll gather at the river,*
> *The beautiful, the beautiful river;*
> *Gather with the saints at the river*
> *That flows by the throne of God!*

On the seventh day of creation "God saw everything that he had made, and behold, it was very good" (Gen 1:31). When the redeemed behold the new heavens and new earth that God prepares for us, we too will say it is *very good*!

We do not know the time for the consummation of the earth and of humanity (cf. Acts 1:7), nor do we know how all things will be transformed. As deformed by sin, the shape of this world will pass away; but we are taught that God is preparing a new dwelling place and a new earth where justice will abide (cf. 2 Cor 5:2; 2 Pet 3:13) and whose blessedness will answer and surpass all the longings for peace which spring up in the human heart (cf. 1 Cor 2:9; Rev 21:4-5). Then, with death overcome, the sons of God will be raised up in Christ, and what was sown in weakness and corruption will be invested with incorruptibility (cf. 1 Cor 15:42, 53). Enduring with charity and its fruits (cf. 1 Cor 13:8; 3:14), all that creation (cf. Rom 8:19-21) which God made on man's account will be unchained from the bondage of vanity.

Therefore, while we are warned that it profits a man nothing if he gain the whole world and lose himself (cf. Lk 9:25), the expectation of a new earth must not weaken but rather stimulate our concern for cultivating this one. For here grows the body of a new human family, a body which even now is able to give some kind of foreshadowing of the new age.

Pastoral Constitution on the Church in the Modern World,
December 7, 1965, No. 39

FOR PERSONAL CONSIDERATION

1. The *Pastoral Constitution on the Church in the Modern World* cited above tells us that we should have a concern for this world even though it is passing away. What practical things can you do to respond to this call of Vatican II?

2. Read the account of the garden in Genesis 1-2. Then read Revelation 21-22. What things are similar in the first and final gardens? What is different?

SECTION II

~

The First Things

"While I thought that I was learning how to live, I have been learning how to die."

Leonardo da Vinci

"Of every one, young and old alike, death makes either a friend or an enemy. To his enemy he is an abiding terror, to his friend he is friend indeed; warning in danger, in trial encouraging with strong hope, reconciling in misfortune, stirring when action is called for, stimulating to every sacrifice."

Most Rev. Alban Goodier, S.J.

CHAPTER 9

Life Before Death

I have always preferred public transportation to driving a car. On a bus or an airplane I can indulge in my two favorite activities: reading and talking with people. One morning as I was headed to my office, I was reading the book *Preparation for Death*, by St. Alphonsus Liguori. In the seat behind me on the bus was a young woman from my neighborhood. As she leaned over the back of my seat she asked, "What are you reading?" In response, I whispered: "*Preparation for Death*." "What did you say?" she asked. I closed the book so that she could see the cover and again whispered, "*Preparation for Death*." In a shocked voice my fellow bus rider yelled, "Preparation for death! — What's wrong with you!" As most of the other riders on the bus turned to look at me, I could read in their questioning eyes, "I wonder if his fatal disease is communicable?" I also then knew that from that day forward I would have a seat alone on the morning bus.

In a very real sense, our entire life is to be a preparation for death, or, more accurately, it is to be a preparation for eternal life. In the first section of this book we took a quick survey of the last things — what we see on the horizon of this life. These are realities more firm than a tree or desk. They are the stuff of life, real life, eternal life. This final life, life with God, is the fulfillment of our deepest hopes and needs. It is a life worth striving to attain. It is worth sacrifice, plan, and purpose.

God has not left us in the dark as to how to attain the life He promises. In the Old Covenant, God spoke to man through the patriarchs, the law, and the prophets. Then, in the New Covenant, God sent His own son, Jesus. He is the Eternal Word spoken in time and He, who is truly God, has shown us the life we are called to live. He not only revealed the way, He is the Way! It is through Him, and only through Him, that we have access to the Father and the kingdom that is to come.

He made the plan of God abundantly clear: "He (Jesus) said to them, 'You are from below, I am from above; you are of this world, I am not of this world. I told you that you would die in your sins, for you will die in your sins unless you believe that I am he'" (Jn 8:23-24).

Life always begins with birth. You were born into this present life on a specific day — a date you celebrate as your "birthday." There is another birth that we are called to embrace. It is a spiritual birth that comes through Jesus.

Now there was a man of the Pharisees, named Nicodemus, a ruler of the Jews. This man came to Jesus by night and said to him, "Rabbi, we know that you are a teacher come from God; for no one can do these signs that you do, unless God is with him." Jesus answered him, "Truly, truly, I say to you, unless one is born anew, he cannot see the kingdom of God." Nicodemus said to him, "How can a man be born when he is old? Can he enter a second time into his mother's womb and be born?" Jesus answered, "Truly, truly, I say to you, unless one is born of water and the Spirit, he cannot enter the kingdom of God. That which is born of the flesh is flesh, and that which is born of the Spirit is spirit." ... Nicodemus said to him, "How can this be?" Jesus answered him ... "No one has ascended into heaven but he who descended from heaven, the Son of man. And as Moses lifted up the serpent in the wilderness, so must the Son of man be lifted up, that whoever believes in him may have eternal life."

Jn 3:1-15

In this second birth that Jesus describes to Nicodemus, we are born into God's family. And there is yet one more birth that we will experience. At our physical death, we will be born into eternal life. For nine months a child develops in the womb of his mother — growing and preparing for physical birth. We do not know our length of time on earth. Some live to old age while others die young. But no matter what the length of time given to us, it is the time to prepare for that final birth into life eternal. There can be no greater tragedy than to miss the promise of God because we were unprepared for this final birth.

There is another aspect to birth; it always involves death to the previous life. The child cannot remain in the mother's womb. He must die to that life to be born to this physical life that we now share. To enter eternal life a person must die physically. In the spiritual life a person must die to self so that he can live in Christ. Death is always a part of birth, and even though the prospect of new life is exciting, the accompanying need to die can be frightening.

In this second section of the book we will look at what is involved in our preparation to be born again as Jesus described to Nicodemus. We will consider what type of death must occur if we are to come to the promised new life. "Behold, now is the acceptable time; behold, now is the day of salvation" (2 Cor 6:2). Now is the time to "make correct judgments about the true meaning and value of temporal things, both in themselves and in their relation to man's final goal."[30]

> **If we understand that what seems to us living is actually dying, we may at last be ready to understand that what seems to us dying is actually living.**
>
> Fr. Richard John Neuhaus
> *Reflections on Dying*, (Notre Dame, IN: University of Notre Dame Press, 2000), 39

> **Yet Lord, instruct us to die,**
> **That all these dyings may be life in death.**
>
> George Herbert, "Mortification"

FOR PERSONAL CONSIDERATION

1. Read Romans 6:8-11. How is a death involved in coming to life?

2. Read Romans 8:11-14. What is the result of the ongoing death to which Paul encourages the Romans and us?

CHAPTER 10

Born into the Family

At some specific time in history, your natural life, outside of your mother's womb, began. And before that actual day of birth, you were undergoing development. Within your mother you were formed and grew. Your organs developed; your features became distinct; even part of your personality was formed. After about nine months of formation, you were ready. The time of birth was at hand. You became an active part of a family, either your natural family or an adopted family. Your life radically changed from the life that you knew in the womb. You left a warm and secure place to enter a new and exciting, but also frightening, world. After birth, your life would never be the same.

This natural birth parallels the spiritual birth that God offers to us. He calls every man and woman to join His eternal family. God is eternally a family because He exists as a Trinity of Persons: Father, Son, and Holy Spirit. Perhaps the most quoted Scripture is: "God is love" (1 Jn 4:8, 16). If God is love now, He has been so for eternity. Love implies relationship, and the love life shared in the Trinity is one of family love. And it is to this eternal family that God invites each of us.

The nature of love is that it is to be shared. A married couple, hopefully, gives their love fully to each other. When, through their love for each other, a child is born and enters that natural family, their love for each other is not decreased. Instead, love expands to include the child, and even the couple's love for each other deepens because they now share a common love for their offspring.

Again there is a parallel with God's love. His love is offered to all men. As people join His family there is an expansion of love. As God's family grows, the effects of that relationship of love become more evident.

God created us to share everlasting family life with Him, and Baptism is the essential means of entering God's family and embracing the possibility of sharing endless life with Him. Since that eternal family life is both our hope and our goal, Baptism, as the gateway into God's family, takes on real significance for us.

But why is Baptism necessary? (cf. CCC 846, 1257). The Church teaches that there is "the necessity of Baptism for salvation" (cf. 1 Tim 2:4) (CCC 1256). In requiring Baptism, the Church is only following the directive of its founder, Jesus Christ, who said to Nicodemus and to all who desire eternal happiness: "Unless one is born of water and the Spirit, he cannot enter the kingdom of God" (Jn 3:4). And Christ explicitly commanded His Church to "[g]o . . . and make disciples of all nations, *baptizing* them in the name of the Father and of the Son and of the Holy Spirit" (Mt 28:19, emphasis added).

Effects of Baptism

What then is the relationship of Baptism with "last things"? The key is that Baptism has eternal consequences because it is our entrance into God's family and is necessary for salvation.[31]

Baptism is a sacrament that can only be received once. In the sacrament of Baptism, a permanent change occurs in the recipient. The *Catechism of the Catholic Church* states: "Incorporated into Christ by Baptism, the person baptized is configured to Christ. Baptism seals the Christian with the indelible spiritual mark (*character*) of his belonging to Christ. No sin can erase this mark" (CCC 1272, emphasis in original).

When a person is conceived and then born into a family, there is something permanent that occurs. I carry the genetic mark from my parents. I may claim that my birth parents are not really my parents, but a DNA test will prove otherwise. I can change my name, move to another state, and dye my hair, but I cannot change the fact that I have a particular mother and a particular father. It is built into my very make-up.

The rebirth in Baptism gives me a new Father — the eternal "Abba" (Gal 4:6) — in heaven. The sacrament gives me a new brother, Jesus. And in and through Him I am related to all of Christ's other brothers and sisters (Rom 8:29).

When I am born into this family, a permanent relationship is established. I can't change the fact that I have been sealed with the blood of the Lamb in Baptism. I may not live the life to which I am called, and I may not respond to the grace that God gives me, but I will continue to bear the family mark. In other words, I can be an unfaithful, ungrateful, lapsed son, but there remains a sort of spiritual DNA that connects me to Christ (CCC 1272-1274).

Recall the Scripture where Jesus tells the story of the prodigal son (Lk 15:11-32). The prodigal tells his father that he wants out of the family: "Give me my inheritance and I'll be on my way. I don't need and don't want this family." It is a done deal as far as the son is concerned. But not so with the Father! He continues to see the prodigal as his son, albeit wayward. Despite the son's lack of respect and gratitude, and despite the fact that the son rejects the lifestyle and morality of the father, the father continues to uphold a familial bond with his son. He is constantly awaiting the son's return. He is on the lookout.

When the son finally realizes the error of his ways, he decides to return to the ancestral home — not as a son, but rather as a hired servant. He realizes that he has broken the relationship, but the father doesn't see it that way. The prodigal is still his son — a sinful child — but certainly a son nonetheless.

This is the effect of Baptism on each of the baptized. Yes we sin; yes we wander; yes some even overtly reject God, but the mark, the seal, the character of Baptism, remains. Repentance and the sacrament of Reconciliation can re-establish an active relationship with our heavenly Father and His family. In fact, our Father is always on the lookout for the prodigal to return. He is always calling His children home and, until our death, we are people of hope. We can choose hell only by obstinately failing to run to the embrace of our Father.

There is no sin bigger than God. There is no distance wider than His arms can reach. He awaits the return of all His wayward children.

This truth — that we posses the spiritual DNA that identifies us as children of God — is not merely a nice concept. Grasping this eternal reality has profound implications for our identity, for how we live our lives, and for how we relate to others. For example, we have a new name that identifies the nature of our relationship with God.

My name is "Regis" and I am extremely grateful that, at my birth, my parents so named me. Regis is the genitive singular of the root Latin word *rex*, which means "king." So my name then means: "son of the king" or "belonging to the king."

Actually, I share this name with all of my fellow Christians for all the baptized are *regis*. We belong to the King. We are princes and princesses in the royal family of God, who owns the cattle on a thousand hills and who knows all the birds of the air (Ps 50:10-11). In the account of creation, Adam and Eve were given authority over all the living things in the garden. It was a royal authority derived from their unique relationship with God — they were made in His image and likeness (Gen 1:28). They were children of the King. Scripture tells us that in the new creation the saints, children of God, will also function with derived royal authority. "Do you not know that the saints will judge the world? . . . Do you not know that we are to judge angels?" (1 Cor 6:2-3).

This is God's plan. We are the King's kids through Baptism. Christ has made a place for us in His Father's house (Jn 14:3). He wants us to be faithful, obedient, and guided by the Counselor, the Holy Spirit, whom the Father sent to lead us into all truth (Jn 14:26). We also have a unique relationship with all of the baptized, whether they are on earth, undergoing purification, or enjoying the fruits of heaven. We are brethren!

This is the truth, and the person with an eternal perspective sees this truth. I may not feel very regal; I may not be experiencing sonship; right now I may feel like punching one of my baptized brothers. The circumstances around me may be distorting the truth of my true family life and leaving me frustrated, angry, battered by temptation, and generally not feeling much like a redeemed son or daughter of the heavenly Father. It is then that an eternal perspective is so important. It is then that I need to look at the ultimate reality, the last things, the things that will last. Regardless of the outward circumstances, if I am in the state of grace, I am an active son or daughter of the King. No exterior circumstances can alter that fact. "I am sure that neither death, nor life, nor angels, nor principalities, nor things present, nor things to come, nor powers, nor height, nor depth, nor anything else in all creation, will be able to separate us from the love of God in Christ Jesus our Lord" (Rom 8:38-39).

When I have the right perspective, it powerfully impacts how I live today. I can avoid an identity crisis if my vision is adjusted to see God's plan. My job may be a mess; I may have cancer; I may be estranged from my children. I will experience the trials and sorrows that accompany these difficulties (note: sonship does not mean freedom from struggle and trial). But, if I keep an eternal perspective, I can stand despite adversity because I am not just any Tom, Dick, or Harry, I am *Regis* — a son of the king! That makes an incredible difference. It is Jesus again who sets the example and shows the way. "Jesus [is] the pioneer and perfecter of our faith, who for the joy that was set before him endured the cross, despising the shame, and is seated at the right hand of the throne of God" (Heb 12:2). We too can endure our crosses with the knowledge that a home is made in heaven for those who are faithful until the end.

Two Brothers

Let's go back to the prodigal son story. While the father embraced the prodigal who had returned home, the older brother had quite a different response. He had been faithful to his father. But he could not accept the mercy of the father (Lk 15:29-30). This prodigal sinner, formerly his brother, was being welcomed back and feasted. We can imagine the older brother whispering under his breath: "Where is justice? My brother left the family."

But as previously mentioned, the baptized always carry the family mark. It is God's intent to bring back the lost sheep, even if it means leaving the rest of the flock for a time (Lk 15:3-6). We need to change our way of thinking and put on the mind of Christ. We are also called to seek the lost and rejoice when a prodigal brother or sister returns to active participation in the family.

There is a temptation for us to think that God is unfair to extend His gracious mercy. But the gospels contain many examples of what we would be tempted to see as unjust. For example, God pays those who worked an hour the same amount that He paid those who worked all day. He rejoices in the return of the lost in a way we are tempted to consider as extravagant. So in the parable where a woman finds a coin that was lost, she invites her neighbors to a party! (Lk 15:8-9).

God is not the only one who rejoices over the return of a prodigal. Scripture says that the angels in heaven rejoice over the return of a lost soul (Lk 15:10). And God expects us to both join in the celebration, as he shows in the parable of the prodigal when he tells the older son to join the festivities, and also to long that the family would be whole. This is the way good families relate. They long to be together and they long to be whole. If we have an eternal perspective, we will see that the baptized are our brothers and sisters in the great family of God. In fact, Christians who are not Catholics but have been validly baptized, are also brothers and sisters, albeit lacking the fullness of truth that is available only in the deposit of faith entrusted to the Catholic Church. The Decree on Ecumenism from Vatican II states: "It remains true that all who have been justified by faith in Baptism are members of Christ's body, and have a right to be called Christian, and so are correctly accepted as brothers by the children of the Catholic Church" (*Unitatis Redintegratio* #3). And so the Church rightly refers to these individuals as "separated brethren."

Responsibilities

Being part of Gods family also comes with responsibilities. You don't expect your next-door neighbor to take responsibilities in your home. But you do expect your children or other family members to take responsibility for the needs of the household. If laundry needs to be done or the porch painted, it is the responsibility of the family to meet the needs.

So it is for us who are members of the family of God. We are expected to participate in the family work. In fact, the needs of the family have a greater priority than many of our personal needs. The head of the family, our heavenly Father, sets the agenda. Christ, our elder brother and example, has shown us how to respond. He says that He does "only what he sees the Father doing; for whatever he does, that the Son does likewise" (Jn 5:19). The Father of the family is working and we are to participate as Jesus does: "My Father is working still, and I am working" (Jn 5:17).

How important is it for us to participate in the family work? Because the work of the Father has eternal consequences, the doing of His will should be paramount in our lives. Those things which are lasting have a greater call on our lives than those things which are fleeting.

Jesus explicitly tells us that we are to work for that which is eternal. "Do not labor for the food which perishes, but for the food which endures to eternal life" (Jn 6:27). When Jesus taught his disciples to pray, he told them to ask the Father to meet their needs by providing their daily bread, but only after first telling them to pray,

> "Thy kingdom come,
> Thy will be done,
> On earth as it is in heaven" (Mt 6: 10).

This radical trust can be a bit unnerving. There can be the fear that if I put the affairs of God's kingdom above my needs, then I am at risk of poverty and the lack of material things. But God anticipates our fears and tells us:

> Do not be anxious about your life, what you shall eat, nor about your body, what you shall put on. For life is more than food, and the body more than clothing. Consider the ravens: they neither sow nor reap, they have neither storehouse nor barn, and yet God feeds them. Of how much more value are you than the birds! And which of you by being anxious can add a cubit to his span of life? If then you are not able to do as small a thing as that, why are you anxious about the rest? Consider the lilies, how they grow; they neither toil nor spin; yet I tell you, even Solomon in all his glory was not arrayed like one of these. But if God so clothes the grass which is alive in the field today and tomorrow is thrown into the oven, how much more will he clothe you, O men of little faith! And do not seek what you are to eat and what you are to drink, nor be of anxious mind. For all the nations of the world seek these things; and your Father knows that you need them. Instead, seek his kingdom, and these things shall be yours as well.
>
> Lk 12:22-31

> If we follow God, heed His call, and remain faithful, we can say to our Lord; "I fear no evil; for thou art with me; thy rod and thy staff, they comfort me."
>
> Ps 23:4

This is radical thinking! Perhaps we will recall the testimony of St. Francis of Assisi who gave up all material possessions — including the clothes on his back — to radically follow Christ. That story of St. Francis tells us that sometimes God does call certain individuals to be a militant witness to the consequences of accepting and living the Gospel. But most of us will not be called to the life of a St. Francis. We are to seek God's will for *our* lives. We are all uniquely called and we are to be good stewards of the gifts and possessions that God gives us. We are to be aware that we are a part of the body of Christ, which has arms, eyes, and fingernails. Not all are called to be eyes or hands, but all are called to function in their role in the body. Also, we must remember that there are different gifts, but all are of use in God's Kingdom (cf. 1 Cor 12).

God's children are called to a variety of vocations and walks of life: husband, wife, parent, professional, doctor, street sweeper, and many other trades and professions. We are to do all of our tasks and assignments as unto God Himself. Paul writes to us: "Whatever your task, work heartily, as serving the Lord and not men, knowing that from the Lord you will receive the inheritance as your reward; you are serving the Lord Christ" (Col 3:23-24). Because we do our work for a higher purpose, we should be the best parent, secretary, or lawyer that we can be.

Whatever our profession, vocation, age, sex — whatever our condition may be — the basic truth remains: We are to live our daily lives as active members of God's family who see that how we live today must fit into God's upward call (Phil 3:14). We are to hold fast to the eternal.

The Practical Living

Daily, we should check on our family relationships. We need to examine our consciences, perhaps each night as part of our evening prayer. "How have I lived out my baptism today? Where have I offended my Father, my brothers, and my sisters? Where have I failed in carrying out the family mission? Where have I, like the prodigal, squandered my inheritance?"

When we identify our failings, we then repent. Like the prodigal we are not worthy to be called son because of our sins, but we also see our Father with arms extended to welcome us back. Putting a robe around our shoulders and a ring on our fingers, He gives us again the grace of sonship. We can again cooperate in the family life and business.

Yet we know that we will probably again forget who we are while we are involved in the affairs of this world. We will tend to grumble, to fight, to live as outcasts, eating the food of pigs (Lk 15:16). We need constant reminders that we are children of the King. In every Catholic church there is such a reminder. As we enter we dip our fingers into the blessed water of the font, we sign ourselves as was done to us at our Baptism, "in the name of the Father, and of the Son, and of the Holy Spirit." Yes, we are members of God's family. No matter where we are, we have hope, dignity, and responsibility. We can whisper to our-selves: "I am not just any Tom, Dick, or Harry. I am a son of the King!"

ON BAPTISM

They descend into the water dead, and they arise alive.

The Shepherd of Hermas

A Son of God fears neither life nor death, because his spiritual life is founded on a sense of divine filia-tion.

St. Josemaría Escrivá, *Furrow* 978

Draw strength from your divine filiation. God is a Father — your Father! — full of warmth and infinite love.

St. Josemaría Escrivá, *Forge* 331

FOR PERSONAL CONSIDERATION

1. Read CCC 846 and 1257. Why are Baptism and the Catholic Church necessary for salvation?

2. Read the story of the prodigal son. Examine your conscience. How have you been like the prodigal? Have you sometimes acted or thought like the older brother? Repent for the times you have failed. Plan to go to the sacrament of Reconciliation, just as the prodigal returned to his father, knowing that your Father awaits you with open arms.

CHAPTER 11

Brothers and Sisters,
Servants and Ambassadors

So, Baptism makes us children of God and part of His family. And a large family it is! Scripture reminds us that God desires all men to come to Him and be saved (2 Pet 3:9). The number of those who have been sealed in Baptism is substantial. And the family is larger than those whom we see on earth today. It includes all those who have lived in the past and who now are in heaven or are undergoing purification in purgatory — a concept that has already been discussed in Chapter 4.

Our relationship to God's children is an eternal relationship because in Christ we are one. Our task in this life is to begin to nurture a right relationship with our brothers and sisters and foster the growth of the family of God. Relationships in the world are difficult. People fear being hurt or used. If I trust someone, if I forgive someone, if I serve another, I run the risk of being hurt, rejected, or used. When my vision is focused only on this life, then the risk involved in trust and love may be too high. If I am only looking out for number one and my expectations of trust and love are not met, I am tempted to retaliate or escape. In marriage that means divorce, in friendships it means separation, between countries it means wars.

But if my perspective is eternal, I know that I am part of a perfected family. Right now, I am in the training stages. This earthly life gives me the opportunity to be formed into a brother or sister to Christ, and, consequently, into a loving brother or sister to all the kids of the kingdom — those who have accepted the gift of salvation and those who hopefully will do so before their death.

Scripture is replete both with teachings on how to relate to fellow Christians and on how to relate to those outside of the faith.[32] And Christ Himself has taught us the manner in which we relate to others. We, who answer to a higher — an eternal — calling, are servants and ambassadors of Christ.

Servants

The example Jesus gave was one on servant leadership. Jesus told His disciples; "The Son of man ... came not to be served but to serve, and to give his life as a ransom for many" (Mk 10:45). And He expects that "whoever [of His disciples] would be great among you must be your servant" (Mk 10:43).

The prevailing approach and attitude in the world is often contrary to Catholic thinking. People who demand "rights" without responsibility or accountability exemplify this attitude. It is seen in songs such as "I Did It My Way." It is epidemic in sports, where football players and other athletes dance and point to themselves when they catch a ball, score a touchdown, or make a basket. It can be seen in the daily paper with the stories of greed, ethnic divisions, and bloody confrontations on neighborhood streets.

As Catholics, we realize that our gifts and talents come from God. And with them comes responsibility. We cannot bury our talents, but rather we use them in service of the King, Jesus (cf. Mt 25:14-30). We do not promote ourselves and our way but, instead, serve the Master. Our cause of celebration is to hear our Master say: "Well done, good and faithful servant" (Mt 25:23).

When each day is done and we examine our consciences, we look soberly at our accomplishments. We repent where we have failed or fallen short in our service. We acknowledge where we have done well and been faithful, while also acknowledging that even our own efforts have God's grace at the foundation, for it is the Holy Spirit that works within us. In our hearts we must learn to agree with those words from the Gospel of Luke: "when you have done all that is commanded you, say, 'We

are unworthy servants; we have only done what was our duty'"
(Lk 17:10).

In the world the protest will be heard that this attitude of
the Catholic is merely a form of low self-esteem. But in response
we can point to the fact that we are children of the King of
heaven and earth. God profoundly and personally loves us.
When we are firmly founded on who we are in Christ, we can
embrace the attitude of a servant, which will free us from jeal-
ousy, envy, and the need for human recognition. Any job or
assignment, no matter how menial, no matter whether done
before the admiring crowd or done in private where no one,
except God, will ever know or see, gives satisfaction and honor
when we have done it for love of Christ. As St. Teresa of Jesus
said: "The Lord does not care so much for the importance of
our works as for the love with which they are done."

We know that among the saints there are those who
appeared great in the eyes of the world, such as King St. Louis,
and there are those, such as St. Thérèse, the Little Flower, who
lived a most humble life and loved God by doing dishes and
cleaning floors. What all saints have in common is that they find
their identity as children of the Father and that they obey His
will and render loving, faithful service.

Attitude Toward Others

People whose minds are on this world must find meaning in
their accomplishments, power, and self-assertiveness because
the things of this world are the center of their lives. But as
Catholic Christians we are to be centered on Christ and *the
eternal*. We are to find our identity, joy, and satisfaction in living to love Him who died for us. Honors and accolades are
meaningless for those who seek to serve only one master, Christ.

The Catholic mind differs from the world not only in how
we view ourselves, but also in how we view others. In general
the world takes a very utilitarian view of people. So businesses
do not usually speak of unique individuals; rather they refer to

"human capital." They place this "human capital" right along-side other capital such as equipment, land, money, and buildings on the balance sheet. Another term often used in business is "human resources." Again, the name betrays the thinking. A business has various resources: money, raw material, supplies, and people. These resources are used to run the business and make a profit. If a resource no longer helps in that process, whether it is a computer or a person, that resource is discarded in favor of a new computer or person that will add "value" to the business. Certainly it is important to note that not everyone in business sees people as capital or resources, but the terms point to an overall mindset that dehumanizes people and reflects the value system in Western culture.

This utilitarian approach is evident in many areas of a culture that marginalizes the elderly, legalizes abortion, and looks favorably on assisted suicide and euthanasia. Babies, the elderly, and the handicapped are not recognized as "useful." So the utilitarian approach to those people is to eliminate or marginalize them and spend time and energy on resources that are more "valuable."

This way of thinking can also be seen in a lack of openness and generosity to having and raising children. Most Western countries have a birth rate below replacement level. Predominate beliefs are that more children will hamper the lifestyle of the parents, that in a large family the children will be adversely affected because they won't have all the material perks that are available to a small family, or that the population growth will negatively impact scarce earthly resources.

In contrast to the worldly view, the Catholic perspective is summarized in the writing of Germain Grisez: "Scripture makes it clear that the life of human persons, made in God's image, is sacred. The ultimate basis for the human body's sacredness lies in this: the Word of God became flesh and calls humankind into bodily solidarity with himself.... Therefore, human life always should be treated with reverence, and every person's life, health, and bodily integrity and inviolability are to be fostered and respected."[33]

Every person, from the tiny embryo to the oldest person, carries the breath of God. All human life is made in His image and finds its source in God the Creator. So, suicide and murder are both wrong because we do not own our life or the life of anyone else. God is the owner of life. The *Catechism of the Catholic Church*, echoing the teaching of Pope John Paul II, questions whether the death penalty can be legitimate in our time. It states that the taking of a human life may be acceptable only within the narrow parameters of legitimate defense (CCC 2263-2267).

In his encyclical, "The Gospel of Life," John Paul II summarizes the Catholic view this way: "*Only God is the Master of Life!*" (EV #55, emphasis in the original).

But the Catholic's respect for life goes far beyond merely avoiding killing or even avoiding harm. Christ died to save all men. And He calls us to the same level of love that he showed. "God shows his love for us in that while we were yet sinners Christ died for us" (Rom 5:8).

No person is beyond the love of Christ and, therefore, beyond our call to love. That includes the driver who cuts us off on the road, the drug addict on the street, the terrorist, and the severely handicapped — i.e., all men and women.

Adrienne von Speyr wrote a most profound sentence in the book, *The Holy Mass*: "It is impossible to meet anyone without acknowledging that blood has also been shed for them."[34]

That truth affects the way we relate to the cashier at the store, the person next to us on the bus, and the people who work for us or for whom we work. The precious blood of Jesus has been shed for each and every individual. We can never look at any person as *just* another individual. Blood has been shed for each and every person, and God calls each and every person to accept His love and join His family now and for eternity. As long as someone is alive, no matter how evil the life, there is hope because Christ's blood has been shed, and God, desiring that all be saved, calls that person to salvation and a relationship that has eternal consequences. Everyone on earth is either a brother or sister, or a potential brother or sister.

Catholic social teaching down through the years has laid out some of the implications of our belief in the sacredness of life and our call to establish what John Paul II has called a "Culture of Life." With our eyes focused on truth that is eternal, we are to be ambassadors of Christ and faithful servants. The eternal Light is to shine through us.

> **It is a serious thing to live in a society of possible gods and goddesses, to remember that the dullest and most uninteresting person you can talk to may one day be a creature which, if you saw it now, you would be strongly tempted to worship, or else a horror and a corruption such as you now meet, if at all, only in a nightmare. All day long we are, in some degree, helping each other to one or the other of these destinations.... There are no ordinary people. You have never talked to a mere mortal. Nations, cultures, arts, civilizations — these are mortal, and their life is to ours as the life of a gnat. But it is immortals whom we joke with, work with, marry, snub, and exploit — immortal horrors or everlasting splendours.**
>
> C.S. Lewis, from *The Weight of Glory*

FOR PERSONAL CONSIDERATION

1. Review your relationships. How practically can you be an ambassador of Christ, spreading His love and truth? Resolve during the coming week to implement part of your plan.

2. Decide on one way that you can serve someone in your family
    or immediate circle of friends. When you perform the service, let
    it be known to you and God alone. Prayerfully join it to the work
    of Christ.

CHAPTER 12

The King and His Kingdom

The kingdom of God is a recurring theme in the New Testament and in the teaching of the Church. It is a reality that is here and now, yet also a reality whose fulfillment is yet to be realized.

In His kingdom, God rules and shepherds His people. He works for their/our good (Rom 8:28). It was God's intention from the beginning of creation to have us live in His kingdom under His sovereign and benevolent reign. We know the many blessings that God gave to our first parents in the Garden of Eden. He walked with them in intimate fellowship. But in that primal garden there was no doubt that God was in charge. He was not only Father and friend; he was also ruler and king. God allowed Adam and Eve to rule in the garden, but only as an extension of His rule. The first couple governed because God had directed them to do so.

He also commanded them not to eat of the "tree of good and evil" (Gen 2:17). We are all familiar with the story: Adam and Eve chose their own way rather than that of the benevolent Ruler and, as a result, sin and suffering entered the world. But the death that they would eventually experience was not initially intended as a punishment. It appears that even our first parents were to undergo some transition in order to enter into the fullness of the life that God had planned. Undoubtedly, it was some form of death. That "death" for our first parents was to be like all death — a birth into a new life.

In *First Comes Love*, Scott Hahn suggests that it was fear of physical death that kept Adam, when tested in the garden, from challenging the satanic snake.[35] Hahn writes that Adam "feared his physical death more than he feared offending God by sin."[36] Physical death is not a curse, but spiritual death certainly is — both for Adam and for us. The central problem in the garden was that Adam and Eve responded to their desire for the fruit of the tree, to the lies of Satan, and, perhaps, to their fears instead of following the King's direct orders.

That was then. What about now? Christ told His disciples that in Him the kingdom had arrived. In His parables Christ shows that kingdom life is a right-now reality. Remember the parable of the wheat and the weeds (Mt 13:24-30)? In this story the kingdom is compared to a field that contains both wheat and weeds. God's word has been planted, and wheat has resulted and is nurtured by grace. But yes, there are the weeds.

The Church is the manifestation of God's kingdom today. The Church is "to proclaim and establish among all peoples the kingdom of Christ and of God, and she is on earth, the seed and the beginning of that kingdom."[37] The Church is the visible expression of God's field today, and we need to be planted in it as wheat for the upcoming harvest. And although the Church represents the kingdom in our midst, it is only a shadow of the final glorious kingdom of Christ to come — the one we don't want to miss. "The Church is the 'people gathered by the unity of the Father, the Son and the Holy Spirit'; she is therefore 'the kingdom of Christ already present in mystery' and constitutes its seed and beginning. The kingdom of God, in fact, has an eschatological dimension: it is a reality present in time, but its full realization will arrive only with the completion or fulfillment of history."[38] God is patient and is using His Church to nurture the wheat. It is His desire and intent to harvest much good wheat through the kingdom that is here and now.

So the kingdom is now and is evident through the Church. We are part of that great field that holds the wheat and the weeds. And it is God who does the planting. It is the Holy Spirit "who gives the human heart grace for repentance and conversion" (cf. Jn 15:26; Acts 2:36-38; John Paul II, DeV 27-

48) (CCC 1433). There is no doubt that it is by God's action that individuals enter the kingdom, but not always directly. God often uses intermediaries to help men turn to God. As stated above, the Church is a delegated planter of faith seed and a cultivator of the field. For 2000 years the Church has proclaimed the Gospel, preserved the truth, and ministered the sacraments. These are kingdom actions.

Up Close and Personal

And this phenomenon is not only in the great mission field of the world, but also in the little fields that make up each of our lives. When we respond to God there is kingdom wheat in our lives, but, for now, we know that the weeds of sinfulness, self-ishness, and lack of trust in God still grow in our hearts — right alongside the wheat. At the end of each of our lives there will be a harvesting. Only good wheat can endure the harvest for heaven, so the weeds need to be removed by burning in the fires of purgatory (see Chapter 3).

So, wheat and the weeds coexist in our lives — in our field. But the field itself — our very being — cannot be ours alone. Only God's property is accepted into the next life. That is why conversion, faith, Baptism, and the life in God's family are so fundamental. God can handle weeds in our life, but only when we have given our life to Him.

The fact that Christ is the King has very practical implications. By our Baptism we come under the lordship of Christ; we are kingdom citizens who both await the full realization of that realm and experience it here and now.

A Catholic perspective, with the eyes of the mind focused on that which is lasting, realizes that as Kingdom citizens we have both rights and responsibilities. We are responsible for that seed that the sower plants in the field of our life. We want to be good soil that bears fruit a hundredfold (Mk 4:8). The first task for kingdom livers is to start with the right perspective.

Who's the Boss?

My 6-year-old granddaughter was spending the day at our home. She was anxious about who would be responsible for her, so she asked: "Who's my boss?" After finding the answer to that question, she informed us: "My dad's the boss at my house." After we politely shook our heads, she then asked the million-dollar question: "Who's the boss at this house?"

We probably all know a home where Dad is the king of the castle or where Mom rules the roost. In some homes, although the parents would be reluctant to admit it, it is the children who actually call the shots. I've even been in homes where it was obvious that the pet was the center of the family.

All these options are inappropriate, and embracing any of them will result in problems. In a Catholic family, the domestic Church (CCC 1655-1658, 2204), Jesus should be the "boss." That requires a decision of the will, and it is not a decision that is made only once. It must be renewed daily, even minute-by-minute. The family throne should always be reserved for the King of the universe.

And that family decision begins with individual decisions. Kingdom living starts, continues, and ends with the personal recognition of the true King. It is easily said, but not always an easy task to implement. Most of us want to be the kings and queens — to sit on the royal throne and have others wait on us. Something in us wants to be director and decision maker. I want "me" to be in charge and I want "my" way. That attitude promotes the use of the most destructive word in any relationship: "mine." Isn't that the word that echoed in the Garden? Adam and Eve could have sung a duet to "I Did It My Way!" Unfortunately, my way is a ticket to disaster. It is a journey into darkness. Meanwhile, God's way is the ticket to life.

Since Jesus is King yesterday, today, and tomorrow, as Catholics who know where this old world is headed, we choose freely to make him King in our lives and families. To do so is to live in reality rather than deception — after all, we can only pretend to rule until death intervenes. The King of the universe, the Alpha and the Omega, waits for us to step aside and invite Him to His rightful place in our lives.

Looking Good

The first fruit of living in reality is perspective. If I forget to put on my glasses, the world is a blur. I can't tell if it is three or one person who is walking toward me. I can't see the curb and I am very likely to fall. But with glasses I gain perspective — I can see you clearly and I know where to walk. When I see life through an eternal perspective — seeing the reality that Christ is the King — I can see with greater clarity.

For instance, many of the things that are valued in this world are passing away. It is foolish to build upon anything that will not last. As Jesus taught His disciples: "A foolish man . . . built his house upon the sand; and the rain fell, and the floods came, and the winds blew and beat against that house, and it fell; and great was the fall of it" (Mt 7:26-27). Living in the world we deal with politics, business, social life, et cetera. And we are called to be witnesses and stewards in all those situations, as men and women who respond to the directions of their heavenly King. But we also remember that fame, fortune, health, and wealth in this world pass away. We are to invest not in the earthly kingdom but in the heavenly one. Jesus calls us to focus on the eternal: "Every one then who hears these words of mine and does them will be like a wise man who built his house upon the rock; and the rain fell, and the floods came, and the winds blew and beat upon that house, but it did not fall, because it had been founded on the rock (Mt 7:24-25).

Implications of Living the Kingdom Life

Angels are good examples of what it means to live with the understanding that God is seated upon the throne. A reading of the book of Revelation reveals that the angels position themselves around the throne of God and worship Him (cf. Rev 7:11). They are attentive to His every directive as shown by their activity in carrying out His will. We are to follow their example. We are to attune our spiritual ears to hear the directives of God and follow them. At first blush that may seem to be a very difficult, even impossible, task. After all, we are not standing around the throne of heaven waiting for the next directive. We live in a world that is full of distractions. The world, our flesh, and the devil negatively affect our thinking. We struggle with concupiscence — desires that are not ordered to God's will.

However, we are not without significant aids in our struggle to follow the King. Recall the story of the beggar, Lazarus, who was in the bosom of Abraham and the wealthy man who was suffering in the fires of hell. The wealthy man wanted to send a message to those on earth. What was Abraham's response? "They have Moses and the prophets; let them hear them" (Lk 16:29).

We too have the words of Moses and the prophets that are readily available to us in sacred Scripture. What we call the Old Testament are words that convicted and directed the Jewish people. It provided a beacon of truth for them. It is to do the same for us in the twenty-first century. And we also have the New Testament, from Matthew to Revelation, to teach and guide us. St. Paul writes to his disciple Timothy, and by extension to us: "All Scripture is inspired by God and profitable for teaching, for reproof, for correction, and for training in righteousness, that the man of God may be complete, equipped for every good work" (2 Tim 3:16-17).

Another source of guidance for us to know and follow God's will is the Holy Spirit, the Paraclete.[39] Jesus tells His disciples that "the Spirit of truth . . . will guide you into all the truth" (Jn 16:13). At Pentecost, the Holy Spirit came upon the assembled disciples and not only gave them the words to speak but also the boldness to do so (cf. Acts 2).

We receive the Holy Spirit in Baptism and a further strengthening in Confirmation (CCC 1285). It is the Spirit who helps us in our weakness (Rom 8:26). We know that He is active in our lives because "no one can say, 'Jesus is Lord,' except by the Holy Spirit" (1 Cor 12:3). Whenever we read Scripture, consider a decision, or make a life change, we should seek the guidance of the Holy Spirit. He is near to us and wants to guide and help us through the Bible, through others, through circumstances, and through the Church.

When Jesus ascended to His Father he not only sent the Holy Spirit, he also empowered the Church to carry on His work and spread His teaching. Jesus told Peter, "I will give you the keys of the kingdom of heaven, and whatever you bind on earth shall be bound in heaven, and whatever you loose on earth shall be loosed in heaven" (Mt 16:19). The Church preserves the teaching of Christ by passing it on from generation to generation. The pope and the bishops are the successors of the Apostles "to whom Christ gave the authority to teach, sanctify, and rule the Church in his name" (CCC, Glossary entry on hierarchy). When we follow the teaching of the Catholic Church, which is guided by the Holy Spirit, we can be sure that we are following the directions of the King. For it is He who established that Church as our earthly guide. In the Catholic Church Christ has truly blessed all who wish to follow His kingly lead:

> The Church is ultimately *one, holy, catholic, and apostolic* in her deepest and ultimate identity, because it is in her that "the Kingdom of heaven," the "Reign of God" (Rev 19:6), already exists and will be fulfilled at the end of time. The kingdom has come in the person of Christ and grows mysteriously in the hearts of those incorporated into him, until its full eschatological manifestation. Then all those he has redeemed and made "holy and blameless before him in love"(Eph 1:4), will be gathered together as the one People of God, the "Bride of the Lamb" (Rev 21:9), "the holy city Jerusalem coming down out of heaven from God, having the glory of God" (Rev 21:10-11). For "the wall of the city had twelve foundations, and on them

the twelve names of the *twelve apostles of the Lamb*" (Rev 21:14).

CCC 865

It is a great task, a high honor, an inexpressible gift: to serve Christ the King and commit time, effort, intelligence, and fervor to make him known, loved, and followed in the certainty that only in Christ — the way, the truth and the life (Jn 14:6) — will society and the individual be able to find the real meaning of existence, the code of authentic values, the correct moral line, the necessary strength in adversities, light and hope with regard to meta-historical realities. If your dignity is great and your mission magnificent, always be ready and joyful to serve Christ the King in any place, at any moment, and in any environment.

Excerpt from homily of Pope John Paul II
Solemnity of Christ the King, Sunday, November 23, 1980

FOR PERSONAL CONSIDERATION

1. Consider your daily life. What are your priorities? Are you advancing the kingdom of God or some other kingdom? What can you do to practically make Jesus more the Lord of your life?

2. In your own words, or using the prayer in the appendix, tell Jesus that He is your king and that you want to serve Him.

3. How well and how often do you use the resources that are available to you so that you will better know God's plan and intention for your life? Commit to reading a portion of Scripture each day and begin each session by asking for the guidance of the Holy Spirit.

CHAPTER 13

The Sacramental Life

Life from an eternal perspective is to be lived with God as our Father, Jesus as our elder brother, the baptized as siblings, and the unbaptized as potential family members. Living the kingdom life to which we are called is no easy task. In fact, it is downright impossible — at least with our own unaided power and ability.

On one occasion Jesus gave the disciples a difficult teaching when He told them how hard it was to enter the kingdom of God: "It is easier for a camel to go through the eye of a needle than for a rich man to enter the kingdom of God" (Mk 10:25). The stunned disciples wondered how it was possible for anyone to be saved. At which point Jesus gave them an answer that is still applicable to us today: "With men it is impossible, but not with God; for all things are possible with God" (Mk 10:27).

God does call us to a great life in and of faith. He sets the standards high, as the apostles rightly observed. God calls us to be nothing less than perfect as our heavenly Father is perfect (Mt 5:48). He knows that we are weakened by sin and tempted by that roving lion, the devil, who seeks to devour us. He understands that the concupiscence of our own fleshly desires and the corrupted condition of the world are drawing us away from God and into sin. God well knows that we contend not against flesh and blood but against principalities and powers (Eph 6:12) that make our lives and efforts to do right seem puny. Our Father knows both the height of the call and the difficulty of the climb. In the face of this we are tempted to say with St. Paul: "Wretched man that I am!" (Rom 7:24). But we can also say with Paul, "I can do all things in him who strengthens me" (Phil

4:13). God provides what we need to live the life to which we are called. He provides His grace.

Grace is needed to grow in all aspects of the faith. The sacraments are the main source of this supernatural favor from God. But what exactly is "grace" and how does it help now on my road to the eternal?

Grace is not magic pixie dust, nor is it God waving a magic wand over someone. No, it is not magic, but it is potent. The *Catechism of the Catholic Church* states: "Grace is *favor*, the *free and undeserved help* that God gives us to respond to his call to become children of God, adoptive sons, partakers of the divine nature and eternal life (cf. Jn 1:12-18; 17:3; Rom 8:14-17; 2 Pet 1:3-4)" (CCC 1996, emphasis in original). So it is first of all the help we need to get into God's family. It flows from the redemption Christ gained for us through His life, death, and resurrection.

If you heard that down the street someone was giving out $1000 bills, you would probably head in that direction — I'd go too! God gives His grace of far greater value than a mere $1000 at every Catholic church near our home through the sacraments. There are sacraments that God gives once but through which the grace continues: Baptism, Confirmation, Holy Orders and Marriage.[40] If we continue with the money analogy, receiving these sacraments can be compared to receiving a bank account where the balance never goes to zero. There is always money – grace — available for our use. These sacraments are truly gifts that keep on giving.

And the grace of the sacraments is more valuable than *any* amount of money. Money can cover our present physical needs, but grace meets our spiritual (and sometimes physical needs). A grace filled life helps us to focus on what is important and helps us to move toward our goal in life — i.e., eternal life.

Then there are sacraments that we can receive more than once. They include Reconciliation, Eucharist, and Anointing of the Sick.

Food for the Journey

We need food and drink to live. Take away food and drink and we will die in a matter of days. At the supper before he died, Jesus gave a unique and eternal food to His disciples when He took bread and said, "This is my body," and He took wine and said, "This is my blood." He then told the disciples to "do this" as an everlasting memorial. Through the Eucharist Jesus is with us "till the end of time." His Body under the appearance of bread is food indeed and His Blood under the appearance of wine is drink indeed. In a homily on the Eucharist, John Paul II said: "'Man shall not live by bread alone, but by every word that proceeds from the mouth of God' (Mt 4:4). This word reaches its highest sacramental expression in the Eucharist, when the bread and wine veil the Food and Drink which Christ has prepared for us through his redemptive Sacrifice."[41]

To live the spiritual life, we need spiritual food. In the Old Testament, it was the temple offerings that connected the people to God. The Levitical priest offered the lamb, bread, and wine of the Old Covenant to God. Often part of what was offered to God was eaten by the people. The connection of God to man was through the sacrifice offered to God and consumed by the people.

In the New Covenant, Jesus is priest, sacrifice, and food. Christ, the Second Person of the Trinity, connects us to God through the sacrificial meal instituted at the Last Supper and consummated on the cross on Calvary.

When we worthily receive the Eucharist, we are joined to Christ. Living within us, He can purify, strengthen, and empower us. That which is impossible for man is possible through Christ living in us. When the Mass ends and the priest bids us to go forth, we do so with confidence for we have been fed with the bread of angels![42]

How can we live as Jesus did? By having Him live in us. How can we do the work of Jesus in the world? By allowing the Eucharistic Lord to live and work through us. How can we live the eternal life starting right now? We are able to do this because in the Eucharist we enter into the eternal. The Mass breaks through the curtain of time (cf. Mk 15:38) allowing us to enter into the heavenly throne room of God. We enter an eternal reality as Christ, the victim, priest, and triumphant king, enters us.

Healing Balm

Food and drink are absolutely necessary to both our spiritual and physical life. But we know that sometimes more is needed. If we become sick — infected by a germ or a virus — we need medical attention to recover our health. If we fall and break a bone, we need a trained professional to reset the bone. As healing begins, we often need therapy to regain strength and mobility.

Again these physical problems and solutions have parallels in the spiritual world. We are susceptible to spiritual germs and viruses — sicknesses such as pride, covetousness, lust, anger, and so on. We also enter into sin that leaves us broken and hampered in our ability to live life in and through God. But, thanks be to God, Christ is also the Divine Physician (Mk 2:17). He can bring us healing and strength. When we avail ourselves of the sacrament of Reconciliation, we are paying a visit to the Divine Physician.

We confess our sins of omission and commission to Him in the person of the priest, who is the hands of the surgeon, Jesus. Christ gives us forgiveness — healing! He gives us grace that strengthens us to go on in the spiritual life. Our penance provides a start of the spiritual rehabilitation that is needed for us to better function in our spiritual lives.[43]

A Second Look at Confirmation

Confirmation was mentioned above as a sacrament that is only received once, but because it bears closely on living with an eternal perspective it is worth a closer examination.

Confirmation is a sacrament that builds upon Baptism. In the Western Church this sacrament is only bestowed when the individual reaches the age of reason and is able to make an adult decision to follow Christ.

Most Catholics are baptized as children. They grow in their faith under the tutelage of their parents and with the aid of the parish and wider church. Confirmation provides the opportunity for the individual to personally ratify his or her baptismal promise. It is the opportunity to stand up and take his place in the adult faith community.

The story of the biblical patriarch Jacob illustrates the process. Jacob was born into a religious family. His father was the patriarch Isaac and his grandfather was Abraham. As you read the story of Jacob's life, it is interesting to note that in the early stages of his life, Jacob spoke only of the "God of Abraham and the God of Isaac" (Gen 27:20, 31:9, 31:42). He was living the faith of his father and grandfather, but he did not claim a personal relationship with God (Gen 28:21). Even God did not speak of a relationship with Jacob, but rather of His relationship with Jacob's father and grandfather (Gen 28:13).

Things changed, however. Jacob was returning to his ancestral lands and was going to meet Esau, his brother, whom he had tricked out of his inheritance. Jacob worried about the reception he might receive from Esau. Was Esau still angry? Would Esau kill Jacob? Jacob had burned his bridges behind him, and it looked like he was headed into a life-threatening situation.

It was during this time of uncertainty that Scripture states that Jacob wrestled with God (Gen 32:24-30). In this wrestling, Jacob was blessed by God (Gen 32:29b). This encounter forever changed Jacob, and the change in Jacob was profound — he didn't "walk" in the same way that he had previously (Gen 32:25). Jacob limped, but relied in a new way upon God. He had the courage to meet Esau. Most importantly, Jacob's relationship with God became more personal (Gen 33:20).

Confirmation is the opportunity to get more personal with God. It is a time to walk in a new way as a mature Catholic.

The grace is given in the sacrament and it remains available. It only requires that the individual respond and personally "wrestle" with his God.

> **Every sacrament gives, in addition to sanctifying grace, a "title" to all the actual graces that the recipient will need to achieve the effects of that sacrament.... It is a promise of help, of power, for the rest of one's life.**
>
> Dom Wulstak Mork, O.S.B
> *Transformed by Grace: Scripture,*
> *Sacraments and Sonship of Christ*

FOR PERSONAL CONSIDERATION

1. Recall your Confirmation. Did you see it as an opportunity to make an adult commitment to Christ and His kingdom? Even if you didn't, it is not too late. Renew that commitment and ask God to make the grace of that sacrament more effective in your life.

2. Read the account of Jacob in Genesis 27-33. In what aspects do you identify with Jacob? In what areas of your life are you wrestling with God? When He wins, your life can be different.

CHAPTER 14

Keeping Your Eyes on the Goal

We are in a race. Athletes need to have a "last things first" approach to be successful. Runners run to win a prize, achieve a personal best time, improve their stamina, or just show that they can do it. Even though the goals may vary, one thing remains constant — there is a goal. No sane person would put themselves through the rigorous workouts that are needed to be an effective runner unless he or she had a goal. Keeping their eyes on the goal, athletes work vigorously, endure pain, control eating, and use a whole host of other less then desirable means so that they reach their goal.

Catholics are in a race to reach the prize of glorious, eternal life with the saints and angels in the heavenly kingdom that will fulfill all the desires of the human heart. The writings of St. Paul often use analogies between athletics and the spiritual life. For example, Paul writes; "Do you not know that in a race all the runners compete, but only one receives the prize? So run that you may obtain it. Every athlete exercises self-control in all things. They do it to receive a perishable wreath, but we an imperishable. Well, I do not run aimlessly, I do not box as one beating the air; but I pommel my body and subdue it, lest after preaching to others I myself should be disqualified" (1 Cor 9:24-27).[44]

Actually, our race has already been won — by Jesus, who has become our means of winning the race. He is the beginning, He is the end (the prize), and He is the means. In a real sense our success is totally dependent on Jesus. The author of the book of Hebrews succinctly summarizes: "Let us run with perseverance the race that is set before us, looking to Jesus the pioneer and perfecter of our faith, who for the joy that was set before him endured the cross, despising the shame, and is seated at the right hand of the throne of God" (Heb 12:1-2).

Jesus offers us the victory laurels, but there is one vital, irreplaceable part that we play in the competition. We need to run! Grace and the activity of the Holy Spirit are irreplaceable for the successful spiritual runner. But "it is not easy for man, wounded by sin. . . . Christ's gift of salvation offers us the grace necessary to persevere in the pursuit of the virtues. Everyone should always ask for this grace of light and strength, frequent the sacraments, [and] *cooperate* with the Holy Spirit" (CCC 1811, emphasis added).

Cooperating with the Holy Spirit

The cooperation we are to give is the work of a lifetime. It is a daily saying "no" to self and "yes" to Jesus. "Lord, Your way and will and not mine." It would easily take another book to cover this topic because it touches the essence of our spiritual life.[45] So here we can have only a quick survey.

Spiritual directors often speak of a "plan of life." Like the Olympic athlete, we need a plan to achieve our spiritual goal. What should I do and what should I avoid to make the most of the time that God has given to me? The answer is the foundation of a person's spiritual life. We have already spoken about the sacraments in the previous chapter. The worthy reception of Eucharist and Reconciliation are vital.

Prayer is perhaps the most important tool in your workout routine. It is communication with God. When we pray we open our lives to our Creator and Savior. Prayer is an opportunity to be formed more into the likeness of Christ. We bring God our concerns and, when open to His word and work, can be properly formed.

Prayer for the serious Catholic is to be as regular and important as breathing. In the Part Four of the *Catechism of the Catholic Church* there is a very helpful treatise on prayer — one well worth reading and meditating upon. The Church encourages us to pray regularly: "The Tradition of the Church proposes to the faithful certain rhythms of praying intended to nourish continual prayer. Some are daily, such as morning and evening prayer, grace before and after meals, the Liturgy of the Hours. Sundays, centered on the Eucharist, are kept holy primarily by prayer. The cycle of the liturgical year and its great feasts are also basic rhythms of the Christian's life of prayer" (CCC 2698).

We must develop the mind of Christ. There is a way of thinking that is in accord with the mind of Christ, as we have been exploring in this book. We are called to grow in understanding the plan of salvation offered to us. Study is important, for it forms our mind and calls our heart. Scripture, as God's word, is the primary source for Christian study. St. Jerome wrote that "ignorance of the Scriptures is ignorance of Christ."[46]

There are many other books that can be helpful in understanding the faith and in being formed in the truth. A regular schedule for the reading of good Catholic books and periodicals is time well spent.

In addition to formation of the mind, the Catholic needs to strive to live a life that is pleasing to God by not only avoiding sin but also living out our call to holiness. Practices such as a daily examination of conscience and regular Confession are very helpful. Also, receiving spiritual direction from a priest or someone who is living a solid Catholic life can help to keep a person accountable and focused on "the prize of the upward call of God in Christ Jesus" (Phil 3:14).

The Catholic faith is something too good not to share, and Christ's disciples are commissioned to spread the good news. This not only can be a blessing to others but also is a means to strengthen the faith of the one who shares the Gospel.

Suffering

One striking similarity in the analogy between athletics and the spiritual life is the aspect of pain and suffering. Paul says that he pommels and subdues his body. Part of making Christ and His will paramount in a person's life is the need to make everything else secondary. The Church encourages the faithful to practice penances, fasting, and sacrifices, and to do these mortifications out of love for Jesus and a desire to draw closer to Him. None of these disciplines are ends in themselves; rather they are means to help us put all things under the authority of Christ. When we prayerfully fast or practice mortification, our actions proclaim: "Jesus, You, Your will, and Your kingdom are more important to me than food and comfort — than any worldly pleasure." Christ challenges us: "He who loves father or mother more than me is not worthy of me; and he who loves son or daughter more than me is not worthy of me; and he who does not take his cross and follow me is not worthy of me" (Mt 10:37-38).

It is not that the things of this earth — family, food, comfort, and so forth — are evil, but rather that Christ and His call are more important. It is imperative to find and keep the right point of view. Joining in the sufferings of Christ is a part of keeping an eternal perspective and sharing in the perspective of Christ "who for the joy that was set before him endured the cross, despising the shame, and is seated at the right hand of the throne of God" (Heb 12:2).

> **Brethren, join in imitating me, and mark those who so live as you have an example in us. For many, of whom I have often told you and now tell you even with tears, live as enemies of the cross of Christ. Their end is destruction, their god is the belly, and they glory in their shame, with minds set on earthly things. But our commonwealth is in heaven, and from it we await a Savior, the Lord Jesus Christ, who will change our lowly body to be like his glorious body, by the power which enables him even to subject all things to himself.**
>
> Phil 3:17-21

FOR PERSONAL CONSIDERATION

1. Read CCC 2720-2724. Are you making use of the types of prayer that are available to you? Tell your heavenly Father of your desire to better know Him through prayer. Ask the Holy Spirit to guide you.

2. If you don't have a time dedicated to prayer each day, make an appointment with God for a specific time each day. He'll be waiting for you, so make sure that you keep that daily appointment.

3. Identify some small sacrifice you can make today — perhaps foregoing dessert or going out of your way to encourage someone. Tell our Lord that you are doing it for love of Him. Ask Him to join your small sacrifice with His and use it for the further establishment of His Kingdom on earth.

CHAPTER 15

Dealing with the Fear of Death and Other Objections

Our premise in the previous chapters has been that looking at the last things — death and beyond — gives us perspective on how to live today.

There are three common objections to looking at death and the life beyond. One argument is that by looking at the last things, the Christian will not deal with the problems of this world. It is summed up in the often repeated phrase: "He is so heavenly minded, that he is no earthly good!" However, the opposite is the reality. When we consider the last things, it refines our focus on life in this world. The person with an eternal perspective has God's priorities. The scriptural injunction is the command to love God with your whole heart, soul, and mind and to love your neighbor as yourself. Historically it has been those most committed to Christ — the saints — who have done the most for the inhabitants of this world. There are the obvious examples of those like Mother Teresa whose ministry was to care for the poorest of the poor. But what may not be as clear to the human mind is that the prayers of many holy men and women have done a mighty work to open the floodgates of God's grace upon mankind.

Because Jesus died for all men, the saint is one who believes that it is impossible to meet anyone for whom blood has not been shed. If Jesus has died for all men, how can the Catholic not love and care for all souls?

At times, the Catholic will have a different agenda than what may be propagated in the secular world. But the latest "fad" cause may not be as important as another less publicized cause. The person who looks with godly eyes will be able to discern between the movements to save the trees or the whales and the work needed to end abortion and foster a culture of life. This is not to demean environmental causes. God did tell man to take care of His creation, and responsible stewardship of the earth's resources should be a concern to Christians. But in the light of eternity the saving of one child's life is of immeasurable greater value than saving a forest of trees.

The person who is striving to see the world and his fellow man through God's eyes will be aware of what is important in life. Of necessity that means judicious use of resources, caring for others' spiritual and physical needs, going the extra mile for one's neighbor, and all of the injunctions that Christ gave his disciples in the words of Scripture.

Morbid

Another objection to our discussion of death and the life beyond is that it is morbid. However, the Christian who is cultivating the eternal perspective is not considering death per se. Instead he looks at death as the gateway to life — eternal life. Morbidity is a focus on the gruesome and the grisly. For the Catholic death is a passage. The particulars of a death may be gruesome, but death is always meant to be life-giving.

If you have witnessed the birth of a child, you know it is possible to describe it as a gruesome and horrible event. There is blood and pain in abundance. Yet the result is a child! That new life gives a whole different perspective to the travail that precedes the birth. Most women, when they hold a new child in their arms, will say that it was worth it.

As mentioned previously, in a real sense death is a birth — final birth. Physical birth involves a significant life change for the child who has lived for nine months within the shelter of the womb. He then makes a journey to a new, strange, but wonderful new life. We know that this child experiences stress, at least physical stress, in the process.

Death parallels this experience. The person for a certain number of years has lived in the womb of this earthly world. It is a known place, a safe place, and one in which the person is reasonably comfortable. Death means a journey from the known to the unknown, and it is stressful. To outward appearance it is pain, blood, and sadness. But if the individual is traveling to the arms of his heavenly Father, the journey is well worth the pain — any amount of pain. To be held in the arms of the Father in the presence of our elder brother Jesus will be joy to a degree beyond any comparison. As St. Paul writes, all else that we have experienced will appear as so much rubbish because of "the surpassing worth of knowing Christ Jesus my Lord" (Phil 3:8).

Fear

The third objection centers on fear. If we begin to discuss death and its personal consequences (we all will face it), some people will experience fear. Fear is a natural reaction to potential danger and the unknown. Fear is a very necessary reaction in the world. It keeps the sane man from walking into a den of hungry tigers or leaning out the window on the thirtieth floor of a building.

Our Lord knew that in the face of death, with the likelihood of pain and a paucity of experiential knowledge of the process, people would experience fear. In fact, ten times in the new testament either Jesus or an angel sent from God brings the message, "Be not afraid!"[47] If it is said so often, then we should take the message seriously.

Our response to the directive to "be not afraid" is to believe that God can be trusted and that we must strive to incorporate trust in God into our thoughts. Little children implicitly trust their parents. Part of our scriptural call to be as little children is to trust our heavenly Father because He will give us what is good for us (Mt 7:9-10). Paul tells us; "We know that in everything God works for good with those who love him" (Rom 8:28). If we abide in Him, He will see us through our trials.

How do we grow to trust God with our physical death? We do it by dying regularly, daily, even hourly. Our physical death is only to be one in a continuum of deaths that we must embrace. We are to die to sin and live in Christ Jesus. In fact the Christian life is a continuing choice to die. I may want to skip Mass on Sunday and play golf. But I realize that Sunday Mass is an obligation incumbent upon me as a Catholic. But even more than an obligation, I know that as creature I need to worship my creator. I also know that Sunday is a little Easter that celebrates the resurrection of the Lord and opens the possibility for my own eventual resurrection. I know too that at Mass I will receive spiritual food — the Body, Blood, Soul, and Divinity of Jesus — that I desperately need to live the life to which God has called me. So I die to self — I say no to that desire for a Sunday golf game and yes to Sunday Mass — a little death that gives an abundance of life? Yes, and it is a training for dying — better said, embracing greater life — in the future.

Consider the ways in which we are called to die — how we are called to say yes to God. As a spouse I must put the needs of my wife above my own. In the work environment I am called to be honest and work as unto the Lord, no matter the personal cost. I am called to stand for truth and justice even when it is unpopular. These little deaths are training us in obedience and trust. This attitude is at the heart of the very prayer that Jesus taught us, His disciples: "Thy will be done."

And, as in all aspects of the Christian life, Jesus has shown us the way. Far before Calvary, Christ had said yes to His Father in all aspects of His life and mission. His entire life was obedience and union with His Father. Perhaps the penultimate example is the agony in the garden. It was a frightful experience in which our Lord literally sweated blood. In His humanity he desired a way other than the one that His Father revealed to Him. And Christ asked: "Father, if thou art willing, remove this cup from me" (Lk 22:42a). But Jesus immediately laid down His desire as He said; "nevertheless not my will, but thine, be done" (Lk 22:42b). Jesus died that moment as surely as he died on Calvary. Death is to say no to self and to fall into the hands of the living God (Heb 10:31). So is it not better and truer to say that in dying we embrace the life offered by our Father?

In Baptism we embrace our first death as a new Christian, but it is indeed a life-giving death. As Paul tells us: "Do you not know that all of us who have been baptized into Christ Jesus were baptized into his death? We were buried therefore with him by baptism into death, so that as Christ was raised from the dead by the glory of the Father, we too might walk in newness of life" (Rom 6:3-4; cf. Col 2:12) (CCC 1227). It is the start of a life where we can willingly die for the greater value of the life offered by Jesus.

There are many Scriptures that support this thesis that, as we meditate on them, can be vital in changing our fear to trust and hope.

> If we have been united with him in a death like his, we shall certainly be united with him in a resurrection like his. We know that our old self was crucified with him so that the sinful body might be destroyed, and we might no longer be enslaved to sin. For he who has died is freed from sin. But if we have died with Christ, we believe that we shall also live with him. For we know that Christ being raised from the dead will never die again; death no longer has dominion over him. The death he died he died to sin, once for all, but the life he lives he lives to God. So you also must consider yourselves dead to sin and alive to God in Christ Jesus.
>
> Rom 6:5-12

> Since therefore the children share in flesh and blood, he himself likewise partook of the same nature, that through death he might destroy him who has the power of death,

that is, the devil, and *deliver all those who through fear of death were subject to lifelong bondage.*

Heb 2:14-15, emphasis added

The Church in her prayers for the deceased reaffirms that we have no reason to fear for "life is changed, not ended. When the body of our earthly dwelling lies in death we gain an everlasting dwelling place in heaven" (Preface, *Christian Death I*).

If you are someone who fears death, first know that you are not alone. But even more know that you can grow in trust that can free you from fear. John the Evangelist writes, that "[t]here is no fear in love, but perfect love casts out fear" (1 John 4:18). It is not that we need to have perfect love in order not to fear. Rather we should know that God who is love drives out our fear. As we draw closer to him, he can sooth our fears. "God is love, and he who abides in love abides in God, and God abides in him. In this is love perfected with us, that we may have confidence for the day of judgment" (1 Jn 4:16-17).

Perhaps as a ready reminder you might want to put this Scripture in a place where you will often see it. "Fear not... for it is your Father's good pleasure to give you the kingdom" (Lk 12:32).

A living hope in life after death . . . determines a responsibility for life here on earth that can make renunciations for the sake of the common good because the brief earthly life is lived as a responsible pilgrimage and is not clung to as the final goal.

Cardinal Christoph Schönborn, *From Death to Life*, 171

FOR PERSONAL CONSIDERATION

1. Do you fear death? Write out the reasons that you should trust God. Make them regular material for reflection in your prayer.

2. St. Peter tells us to "be prepared to make a defense to any one who calls you to account for the hope that is in you" (1 Pet 3:15). Review how the eternal perspective actually enables Catholics to be better citizens of this world so that you can convey this truth to others.

SECTION III

The Transition:
From Life to Life

"I am not dying; I am entering into life."

St. Thérèse of Lisieux, quoted in *Catholic Book of the Dead,*
by Ann Ball (Huntington, IN: Our Sunday Visitor, 1995), p. 186

CHAPTER 16

From Life to Life

In the first section of this book we examined the things of eternity, the reality that lies on the far side of the grave. In the second section we looked at present reality and examined how we should live this life knowing the reality of the eternal life. Now it is time to discuss the transition from the temporal to the eternal.

In general, cultures have developed rituals to surround death. Even lacking the revealed truth of Christianity, man has seen fit to approach death with a certain wonder and awe. Death is a most natural process. The body wears out and ceases to function. It then, in the normal course of events, undergoes decay until eventually there are only bones or less.

But men do not treat death in the same manner as animals. It is a sign of the inner knowledge of man that, despite the "naturalism" of death, he treats the body of the deceased with respect. Human life has value. The body was part of a unique person and is deserving of respect in death. It is true that throughout history there have been those who have disrespected the bodies of the deceased. Yet tyrants, while disregarding the value of other life, still build edifices for their mortal remains. In essence, they still see the value of the person but relegate that value to a distinct few.

Scripture severely criticizes those who fail to bury the dead. Meanwhile, those who reverently and faithfully bury the dead are praised. Tobit is identified as a just man because he took concern to bury the dead even when it put his life in danger:

In the days of Shalmaneser I performed many acts of charity to my brethren. I would give my bread to the hungry and my clothing to the naked; and if I saw any one of my people dead and thrown out behind the wall of Nineveh, I would bury him. And if Sennacherib the king put to death any who came fleeing from Judea, I buried them secretly. For in his anger he put many to death. When the bodies were sought by the king, they were not found. Then one of the men of Nineveh went and informed the king about me, that I was burying them; so I hid myself. When I learned that I was being searched for, to be put to death, I left home in fear. Then all my property was confiscated and nothing was left to me except my wife Anna and my son Tobias.

Tob 1:16-20

Not to be properly buried was seen as a curse. As recorded in the Second Book of the Maccabees, Menelaus had abused the people and ignored God. His lack of burial was seen as fitting for his crimes. "Menelaus the lawbreaker died, without even burial in the earth. And this was eminently just; because he had committed many sins against the altar whose fire and ashes were holy, he met his death in ashes" (2 Mac 13:7-8).

Appropriate grieving and a dignified burial are responsibilities that a pious man should not ignore. The author of Sirach writes: "My son, let your tears fall for the dead, and as one who is suffering grievously begin the lament. Lay out his body with the honor due him, and do not neglect his burial" (Sir 38:16).

While all societies develop ritual for the deceased, the Jewish and Catholic faiths are extraordinary in understanding the transition that occurs for the individual at death. Both Jews and Catholics have established and maintained cemeteries from ancient times up to the present. We can still visit the burial places of early Christians in the catacombs in Rome and in other locations.

The Church in Canon law has identified two types of places as sacred — places set aside for a holy purpose. One such place is the church building, which is specifically blessed by the bishop of the diocese and dedicated for a sacred use. Mass will be offered there and Jesus will be truly present on the altar and in the tabernacle when the sacred species is reserved there. If a Church is to be abandoned, there is a special decommissioning service.

The other place that Canon Law identifies as sacred is the Catholic cemetery. Here the bodies of the saints will lie in rest until they are called forth at the end of time in the Resurrection of the Body. The physical remains of a Catholic who is buried in a cemetery have been an integral part of a unique person. That body was a tabernacle that held the Body, Blood, Soul, and Divinity of Christ (in a way no less than that gold tabernacle in a Church) when that person received Communion. That body was also sealed with the waters of Baptism and became a temple of the Holy Spirit.

Needless to say, the Church sees the death of one of the faithful as a most significant event. It is transition from one life to another. It is the time when he who has been born again in the waters of Baptism now experiences a final birth into eternal life. It is the fulfillment of a promise for those who have placed their faith in Christ.

The Church provides a perspective of faith, hope, and love to those who are dealing with death. She also dispenses the graces of Christ. Let us then look at what the church teaches about this most important time of life — death. Let us also examine the blessed grace that is available from the storehouse of grace that Christ has entrusted to His Church.

> **Through eternity what is transitory acquires meaning, and death becomes an element of life, man's way to going to God.**
>
> Adrienne von Speyr, *The Mystery of Death*, 35

FOR PERSONAL CONSIDERATION

1. What are your ethnic, cultural, and family rituals surrounding death and burial? Do they affirm the Catholic understanding?

2. Why does Jewish tradition, as seen in the Old Testament, place such emphasis on the proper burial of the deceased? (See Gen 23:4-20; 50:13-14; Eccles 6:3; Sir 38:16.)

CHAPTER 17

Anointing of the Sick

The Anointing of the Sick is one of the seven sacraments. The *Catechism of the Catholic Church* gives a succinct definition for this sacrament — a definition worth contemplating. "The sacrament of Anointing of the Sick has as its purpose the conferral of a special grace on the Christian experiencing the difficulties inherent in the condition of grave illness or old age" (CCC 1527).

One of the Scriptures that provides background to the Anointing of the Sick is found in the Letter of James: "Is any among you sick? Let him call for the elders of the church, and let them pray over him, anointing him with oil in the name of the Lord; and the prayer of faith will save the sick man, and the Lord will raise him up; and if he has committed sins, he will be forgiven" (Jas 5:14-15).

The sacrament is for anyone who is seriously ill.[48] The prayers of this sacrament certainly ask for healing. The minister of the sacrament, a priest or bishop, prays that the Lord would "save" and "raise up" the ill person. That healing may be physical, but the prayer also has a more profound meaning. Ultimately the "saving" that is most necessary is the salvation that leads to eternal life with God. The "raising up" that is most necessary is that which is joined with the resurrection of Jesus and leads the soul of the individual into the eternal kingdom of God.

Since sin is the barrier that stands between the sick person and union with God, prayers are offered for the forgiveness of sin.

Whenever possible, two other sacraments are offered to the sick person, especially if the individual is gravely ill and in danger of death. The priest will offer the person the opportunity to receive the sacrament of Reconciliation. Again, freedom from sin opens the door to grace and life.

In addition, the priest will make Communion available to the person if the individual is physically able to receive our Eucharistic Lord. Communion given to a dying person is referred to as "*Viaticum*." It is food for that final journey from transitory life to eternal life through the conduit of death. The *Catechism of the Catholic Church* states:

> Communion in the body and blood of Christ, received at this moment of "passing over" to the Father, has a particular significance and importance. It is the seed of eternal life and the power of resurrection, according to the words of the Lord: "He who eats my flesh and drinks my blood has eternal life, and I will raise him up at the last day" (Jn 6:54). The sacrament of Christ once dead and now risen, the Eucharist is here the sacrament of passing over from death to life, from this world to the Father (cf. Jn 13:1).
>
> CCC 1524

Since Vatican II there has been a renewed emphasis on the communal nature of this sacrament. Anyone who is present during the anointing is invited to also pray for the person who is sick. The prayers of those present are united with the prayers of the entire Body of Christ, especially those of the saints (cf. CCC 1516, 1522).

The definition of a sacrament, which began our discussion, states that grace is made present for the person who receives the sacrament.

The grace particular to this sacrament is "one of strengthening, peace and courage to overcome difficulties that go with the condition of serious illness." The Holy Spirit also aids the recipient by a renewed "trust and faith in God and strengthens against the temptations of the evil one, the temptation to discouragement and anguish in the face of death" (cf. Heb 2:15) (CCC 1520).

The person who receives the sacrament is not to be passive. The fruit of the Anointing is in proportion to the openness and disposition of the individual. So, the individual should join his sufferings to those of Christ, seeing in this union with the suffering and death of Christ the sure path to resurrection. As a person yields to grace and actively places himself into the arms of Christ, the Church itself benefits. The sting of death is blunted in the light of the truth of Christ. Death, which had been used as a tool of Satan, is transformed into a door that will open to the home prepared for us by Christ.

The Church is present at the beginning of the physical life of the person and offers Baptism — entrance into the family of God. In the sacrament of the Anointing of the Sick, the Church is also present as physical life draws to an end and offers this anointing to prepare the soul for life with the heavenly Father.

By the sacred anointing of the sick and the prayer of the priests the whole Church commends those who are ill to the suffering and glorified Lord, that he may raise them up and save them. And indeed she exhorts them to contribute to the good of the People of God by freely uniting themselves to the Passion and death of Christ (LG 11; cf. Jas 5:14-16; Rom 8:17; Col 1:24; 2 Tim 2:11-12; 1 Pet 4:13).

CCC 1499

FOR PERSONAL CONSIDERATION

1. Have you ever participated in the Anointing of the Sick? Did you find comfort and support in this sacrament?

2. The Church identifies the Anointing of the Sick as a "communal celebration" even if it is celebrated in a "family home" (CCC 1517). Why does the Church emphasize this communal aspect?

CHAPTER 18

The Catholic Funeral
and Burial Rite

In 1970, at the direction of Pope Paul VI, a revised rite[49] for the celebration of Catholic funerals was promulgated. "Celebration" at first glance may seem to be an inappropriate term to attach to a funeral. In fact, prior to the revised *Order of Christian Funerals* (OCF) the emphasis was on sadness and concern for the sinfulness of the deceased. Certainly prayers for the deceased are very necessary, and there is sorrow at the physical separation from a loved one;[50] nonetheless, the Church also embraces an attitude of joy and hope. For example, prior to the liturgical changes to the funeral rite, black was the color that was worn at the Funeral Mass and was a testimony to the somber mood. Now white, which implies our Christian joy because of the Resurrection, is the color most often worn by the priest for a Funeral Mass.[51]

Also, the pall, the large cloth that covers a casket during a Funeral Mass, is now white. It harkens back to another white garment that was draped upon the individual, now deceased, at his Baptism. Baptism brought the person into God's family when original sin was wiped clean from the soul and the individual was marked as belonging to Christ. Baptism is a burial into the death of Christ so that the person can also rise with Christ. The hope and the promise of Baptism is what we rely upon at death.

The prayers of the OCF are replete with references to the connection between Baptism and death. One of the intercessions for morning prayer in the Office for the Dead is representative:

"Father, through baptism we have been buried with your Son and have risen with him in the resurrection; grant that we may walk in newness of life so that when we die, we may live with Christ forever."

The funeral rite is divided into three main "stages." We recognize that life is a journey — a pilgrimage. The goal of the journey is the beatific vision and eternal life with our Father. The Church, including both the members here on earth and those in heaven, accompanies us on that journey. The OCF gives us another opportunity to walk as a community of faith with the deceased and the surviving family and friends. The three major divisions of the OCF relate to major stops along that road.

The first rite, or stage, that the Church offers is the prayers that follow after death and include prayers that can be said immediately after the death as well as prayers that can be said at the funeral home, or wherever the body lies in repose before the Funeral Mass and subsequent burial. The "Vigil for the Deceased" is a time when the Christian community and the friends and family of the deceased pray and keep watch together. It is a time to support one another and reflect on the mercy of God and the strength that He gives to His brothers and sisters. The Vigil consists of four parts:

- The introductory rites
- The liturgy of the word, which can include a homily
- Prayers of intercession
- A concluding rite and blessing.

A priest or deacon will often lead the Vigil, but a layperson, with slight modification of the rite, can also preside. The Church community is also encouraged to join the family in the celebration.

The scriptural readings are on the theme of eternal life (for example, 1 Cor 5:1, 6-10; and Lk 12:35-40). The intercessions ask the Lord for grace and comfort. One of the concluding prayers summarizes the focus of the Vigil:

Lord Jesus, our Redeemer,
you willingly give yourself up to death,
so that all might be saved and pass from death to life.
We humbly ask you to comfort your servants in their
    grief
and to receive [name of deceased] into the arms of
    mercy.
You alone are the Holy One
you are mercy itself;
by dying you unlocked the gates of life
for those who believe in you.
Forgive [name of deceased] his/her sins,
and grant him/her a place of happiness, light, and peace
in the kingdom of your glory for ever and ever.
Amen

OCF 80

Funeral Mass

The next major stop is the Funeral Mass. The Mass is the most fitting and powerful of prayers and can be offered for the intention of the deceased person. It is a sign of our unity, for in the Mass we enter into something that is eternal. The Mass, which we celebrate in our churches, is a re-presentation of the sacrifice of Calvary. The suffering, death, and resurrection of Christ are the means of salvation — both for us and for the deceased. Indeed, "there is salvation in no one else, for there is no other name under heaven given among men by which we must be saved" (Acts 4:12).

Many sacramentals[52] are used within the funeral liturgy to remind us of various aspects of the journey to eternal life.

The large candle that was blessed on Easter is set at the head of the casket. That candle was first lit at the Easter Vigil as a symbol of the risen Christ who is the light of the world. At the beginning of the Easter Vigil Mass, the Church had been in darkness as it awaited the Risen Lord. The Easter candle had brought light to the darkness. In Christ, darkness is banished and new life is seen in His light. That Paschal light also reminds everyone in attendance that our sorrow must always be tempered by the joy and hope we have in Christ.

The Easter candle is also another reminder of Baptism, for a similar Paschal candle was present at the individual's Baptism. The family life of the Trinity, entered at Baptism, comes to a new level of intimacy in death.

Holy Water is also used at the Funeral Mass as well as at the Vigil service and later at the committal. It too is a sign of Baptism — the waters of salvation. The sprinkling is a form of farewell, while also an acknowledgement of the unity of all the baptized in the Body of Christ.

Incense is often also used during the funeral liturgy. It reminds those present that they can pray for the deceased and that those prayers rise to the throne of God as a sweet fragrant offering (cf. Rev 8:2-4).

Committal

The final phase of a Catholic funeral is the "Rite of Committal." This usually takes place at the cemetery where the body of the faithful departed will be laid to rest.[53] This is the final farewell to the body but not to the relationship with the person if they are destined for purgatory or heaven.

At the beginning of the committal there is an invitation by the minister: "Our brother/sister [name] has gone to his/her rest in the peace of Christ. May the Lord now welcome him/her to the table of God's children in heaven. With faith and hope in eternal life, let us assist him/her with our prayers" (OCF 216).

The service includes the committal prayer, which can take several forms. One such prayer focuses attention on hope: "In sure and certain hope of the resurrection to eternal life through our Lord Jesus Christ, we commend to Almighty God our brother/sister" (OCF 219B). This is followed by intercessions that conclude with the Our Father and a final prayer for the deceased. This service ends with the minister offering a prayer for the surviving friends and family that they would have strength, hope, and comfort in Christ.

Cemetery

Even the cemetery is to be a sign of Christian hope. Only three major religions have made the cemetery a central part of their faith: Jewish, Catholic, and Orthodox. The Catholic Church has maintained cemeteries because of the belief that even in death the body should be treated with respect. A cemetery is identified as "Catholic" if the local bishop or his designee has blessed it specifically for the burial of Catholics. Burial in a Catholic cemetery continues the sense of community that is apparent in the parish and diocesan structure. Catholic cemeteries have been called the "reliquaries of the saints" and the place where the bodies of the faithful rest awaiting the Resurrection of the Dead.

It is not a requirement for the faithful to be buried in a Catholic cemetery. When burial occurs in another cemetery, the priest, or other presider at the committal, blesses the specific grave or crypt where the burial will occur, for it will receive a temple of the Holy Spirit — the body of the Christian.

Intercession for [the deceased] is expressed in various ways, among which is also a visit to the cemetery. To visit these holy places is a propitious occasion to reflect on the meaning of earthly life and to nourish, at the same time, hope in the blessed eternity of Paradise.

Pope John Paul II
Angelus, All Souls Day, November 2, 2003

> Whatever its efficacy may be for the dead, [ritual] binds me up in the bundle of life, situates me in procession of generations, frees me from the prison of here and now.
>
> Milton Himmelfarb
> "Going to Shul" from *The Eternal Pity*, 166

FOR PERSONAL CONSIDERATION

1. What are some of the practical and spiritual benefits of the funeral liturgy for the surviving family and friends?

2. Visit a Catholic cemetery, pray for the deceased, and consider how the cemetery is a silent witness to hope.

CHAPTER 19

The Particular Judgment

At the death of each person his salvation is sealed. Life on this earth is the time to get right with God. If the individual accepts Christ and the salvation He offers, and lives the commands He entrusted to the Church, he will be saved. If a person has rejected God and instead lived for self, he has, in effect, chosen a life in hell.

Each person will receive his reward "immediately after death in accordance with his works and faith" (CCC 1021). This teaching of the Church is affirmed in the letter to the Hebrews: "It is appointed for men to die once, and after that comes judgment" (Heb 9:27). This is called the particular judgment — the judgment rendered for each individual, as opposed to the general judgment at the end of time when all will be judged.

As we have already explored,[54] at this judgment there are three possible results: entrance into blessedness of heaven through a purification; entrance into the blessedness of heaven immediately; or immediate and everlasting damnation (CCC 1022).

This should give everyone a certain urgency to live life according to God's call and, as this book has emphasized, with an eye to the eternal — with an eternal perspective. The prophet Isaiah gives us an encouragement: "Seek the LORD while he may be found, call upon him while he is near; let the wicked forsake his way, and the unrighteous man his thoughts; let him return to the LORD, that he may have mercy on him, and to our God, for he will abundantly pardon" (Is 55:6-7). To be found "in Christ" at the day of our death is to be prepared for one's particular judgment. This is not a position that should be taken for granted. A Catholic's life should be marked by a deep love for Christ, His Church, and for one's neighbors. Nevertheless there is healthy "selfishness" that should drive us to live for and love God — we want to live in God's kingdom fully experiencing the life to which we are called as men and women created "to know Him, to love Him, and to serve Him in this world, and to be happy with Him for ever in heaven."[55]

Another virtue that develops in a person with an eternal perspective is "fear of the Lord." This fear is identified as a gift of the Spirit (cf. Is 11:2). The book of Sirach identifies it as "the beginning of wisdom." This fear is far different from a fear of heights or of tight places. Fear of God comes from an understanding of who God is and of His relationship to man.

It is "a fear in which the element of reverence is uppermost" and it includes "the desire not to offend."[56] God is God, and we are creatures. It is not healthy to confuse the two. Unfortunately too many live this life as if they are God — an approach that can only have eternal negative repercussions.

God is perfect. He is merciful and just. His justice is perfect and his mercy is perfect. We have difficulty with the two concepts co-existing. We tend to believe that justice rules out mercy and that the reciprocal is also true.

Fear of the Lord recognizes both the mercy of God and the justice of God. Fr. John Hardon gives an excellent definition that is worth quoting at length:

> Fear of the Lord . . . confirms the virtue of hope and impels a man to a profound respect for the majesty of God. Its correlative effects are protection from sin through dread of offending the Lord, and a strong confidence in the power of his help.
>
> Unlike worldly or servile fear, the gift of fear is filial because [it is] based on the selfless love of God, whom it dreads to offend. In servile fear, the evil dreaded is punishment; in filial, it is the fear of offending God. Both

kinds may proceed from the love of God, but filial fear is par excellence inspired by perfect charity and, in that sense, inseparable from divine love. When I dread the loss of heaven and the pains of hell, my fear, though servile, is basically motivated by the love of God, whom I am afraid of losing by my sins, since heaven is the possession of God, and hell is the loss of him for eternity. To that extent, even servile fear cannot be separated from supernatural charity. On a higher plane, however, when the object of my fear is not personal loss, though it be heaven, but injury to the divine majesty, then the motive is not only an implicit love of God, but also love to a sublime degree. And this is the scope of the infused gift of the fear of the Lord.

Consequently, the gift of fear gives us the power to sublimate all lesser fears, including the salutary and much-needed dread of God's justice. In the measure that this gift becomes active through generous co-operation, a person comes closer to realizing the ideal of the Christian life, that charity casts out fear. His love of God becomes so intense that gradually the dominant disposition is to fear losing the least spark of God's friendship; and as he grows in charity, the dread of God's punishments flows into a calm assurance of ultimate salvation, and even a strong desire, like Saint Paul's, to be dissolved and to be with Christ.[57]

God extends to each person the grace to know, love, and serve Him. In fact, it is only by the action of God that this is possible. But the free gift of grace requires a response from us since God is always a perfect gentleman. He knocks but always waits for us to open our door. But when we do open to Him, He is most gracious. "If any one hears my voice and opens the door, I will come in to him and eat with him, and he with me" (Rev 3:20).

> The fear of the Lord is glory and exultation,
>   and gladness and a crown of rejoicing.
> The fear of the Lord delights the heart,
>   and gives gladness and joy and long life.
> With him who fears the Lord it will go well at the
>   end;
>   on the day of his death he will be blessed.
>
> Sir 1:11-13

FOR PERSONAL CONSIDERATION

1. Examine your conscience. If you died today, would you be ready to stand before the throne of God? Repent where needed and seek the sacrament of Reconciliation.

2. Consider how you can cultivate a healthy "fear of God" in your life. Read again and meditate on the above definition from Father Hardon. Ask the Holy Spirit to fill you with this godly fear.

SECTION IV

⌒

Helping Others to an Eternal Perspective

"It is, I think, that we are all so alone in what lies deepest in our souls, so unable to find the words and perhaps the courage to speak with unlocked hearts, that we do not know at all that it is the same with others."

Sheldon Vanauken, *A Severe Mercy*

"God presents to us the people and opportunities upon which he expects us to act. He expects no more of us, but he will accept nothing less of us."

Fr. Walter J. Ciszek, S.J., *He Leadeth Me*

CHAPTER 20

How to Help Others Prepare for Death

I knew Tom[58] because we worked together on the board of a Catholic organization. Although he was considerably older than I, we had much in common. For instance, we both were a little neurotic about always being on time. Thus for most meetings we were the first to arrive — at least fifteen minutes in advance of the start. This gave us frequent opportunities to talk. I knew that he was fighting cancer; so it came as no surprise when I heard that his health had taken a turn for the worse.

When I visited him at his home, I found him in a hospital bed in the living room. We chatted about some mutual concerns. He even joked about his condition. After a silence in the conversation, I asked Tom if he was spiritually ready to die. He surprised me when, quickly grabbing my arm and looking me in the eye, he said, "Thank you, no one will talk to me about dying, especially my family. They won't even let me call a priest."

Tom knew he was dying and was struggling to come to grips with that reality. He needed to talk about many issues including the care of his wife, the funeral arrangements, and many practical issues about finances and care of their home. But those closest to him refused to discuss his death. Most importantly, Tom wanted to make sure that he was ready to meet his Maker. But the subject of death was a taboo. Whether because of denial or out of a sense of not wanting to "upset" Tom, his family avoided the subject.

All of Tom's deepest feelings, hopes, and fears were bottled up inside and out of bounds for those he loved.

I made arrangements for a priest to visit Tom, and Father administered the sacraments. He talked with Tom and the family. I don't know what transpired in those conversations, but less than a week later Tom died in peace.

Too often we avoid the discussion of death, even when it stands at the doorstep of our home and is knocking. The most common reason is a desire not to upset the seriously ill person. But this is no service to the dying. An eternal perspective always keeps death and eternal life as a focus, knowing this life is fleeting and that our home is not here.

This life is for building a relationship with Christ and with the people He loves — at least with those whom we encounter during our earthly sojourn. We are here to prepare for the next life. To ignore the eternal is to make the present devoid of meaning. So, then, how do we treat death and how do we relate to those who are dying?

Personal Orientation

First, we need to do a bit of personal reflection. Does my life reflect the fact that I believe in all those phrases that I proclaim in the creed? Do I live as a child of God? Does my life differ from those who live only for today and for self with a disregard for eternal truths?

THE NICENE CREED

We believe in one God,
    the Father, the Almighty,
    maker of heaven and earth,
    of all that is, seen and unseen.
We believe in one Lord, Jesus Christ,
    the only Son of God,
    eternally begotten of the Father,
    God from God, Light from Light,
    true God from true God,
    begotten, not made, one in Being with the Father.

Through him all things were made.
For us and our salvation
 he came down from heaven:
by the power of the Holy Spirit
 he was born of the Virgin Mary, and became man.
For our sake he was crucified under Pontius Pilate;
 he suffered, died, and was buried.
 On the third day he rose again
  in fulfillment of the Scriptures;
 he ascended into heaven
  and is seated at the right hand of the Father.
He will come again in glory to judge the living and the dead,
 and his kingdom will have no end.
We believe in the Holy Spirit, the Lord, the giver of life,
 who proceeds from the Father and the Son.
 With the Father and the Son he is worshiped and
 glorified.
 He has spoken through the Prophets.
We believe in one holy catholic and apostolic Church.
We acknowledge one baptism for the forgiveness of sins.
We look for the resurrection of the dead,
  and the life of the world to come. Amen.

Do my words reflect my belief in the truths of the creed? Are my concerns always focused on the temporal, or do I think and speak from a perspective that the present time is fleeting? Does my Catholic perspective affect my decisions? Where is my treasure and does my heart find peace in the knowledge that by my baptism I have been sealed for Christ (cf. Lk 12:34)?

Evangelist

Vatican II challenged Catholic laity to be leaven in the world. The laity "exercises the apostolate... by their activity directed to the evangelization and sanctification of men and to the penetrating and perfecting of the temporal order through the spirit of the Gospel. In this way, their temporal activity openly bears witness to Christ and promotes the salvation of men."[59] As laity, we are to help those we meet to catch a glimpse of the life that Jesus promises and to which He calls all men. By our words and actions we are to be proclaimers of good news. While those around us may be focused on the ephemeral, we need to point to a reality that is eternal. While others are lost among the "trees," we need to turn their eyes to the road that leads away from confusion to freedom.

The work of being an evangelist is a life-long activity. While people see only darkly (cf. 1 Cor 13:12), we need to make the face of the risen Christ apparent. Having an eternal perspective, we are to show it to others by helping them to understand that knowing the last things will help them to better understand the present.

When Death Calls

So, if we live life with an eternal perspective, we will see death in context. It is a transition, and before death is the time to prepare for birth into eternal life. This means that when someone is seriously ill and in danger of death, we do not hide the truth. Instead we help others to face it with a right perspective.

To ignore eternal realities in the hopes of not worrying or upsetting someone makes no sense. It is better to risk causing some temporary discomfort, if the result will be eternal happiness. This does not mean that we need to preach fire and brimstone to someone who is dying. It does mean that we are to speak the truth in love.

We can also pray and offer sacrifices for the seriously ill person, asking that the Holy Spirit would use the time left to the person to draw him closer to God — to bring repentance, healing, and hope where it may be needed. Also, we should help the person to reconcile (if needed) with the Church, and also to receive the sacraments of Reconciliation, Eucharist, and Anointing of the Sick.

It can also be a time to help friends and family of the deceased to gain a better perspective on life, death, and eternal life. Knowing that death is approaching and having time to prepare is a great grace. Catholics through the ages have asked God to preserve them from an untimely death — a death that gave no time to prepare. The time before death is a time for the Holy Spirit to work. It is a time for those who are separated to return to union with Christ, a time for those who have stains of sin and selfishness to begin the purification process and so to enter more worthily into God's presence. It is a time for the devout to offer their pain and suffering for the needs of others.

As we have discussed in the pages of this book, an eternal perspective makes a tremendous difference in how we live and experience this life. It opens our hearts and minds to things that are truly important. A right perspective means that, despite circumstances, we can still live with joy and peace. And if that perspective makes sense out of life, it certainly makes sense out of death.

So, we should look for opportunities to help those who are dying to prepare for death, asking the Holy Spirit to give us the time and the words we need.

On any number of occasions people have told me that they don't know if they should speak to the dying person about the impending death. Even after asking the Holy Spirit for guidance, they remain unsure and so they hesitate. While it is important to seek guidance, it is better to err on the side of sharing the truth than on not sharing it. Death, no matter how close we may be to God and no matter how often we have had to deal with it, is still an emotional and difficult time. But we are evangelists, ambassadors, and children of the heavenly Father. The *Decree on the Apostolate of the Laity* from Vatican II tells us that we have both the "right" and the "duty" to reach out to others with the love and the truth of Christ.[60]

Rather than fear we should see an opportunity to share eternal truth with the dying and to give them the opportunity to receive the sacraments as a great honor and privilege. Also, remember not to wait. To share sooner rather than later is better, for it gives the individual time to respond and experience God's grace and a happy death.

Behold, now is the acceptable time; behold, now is the day of salvation.

2 Cor 6:2b

Kindly and firmly, family members, friends, and health care personnel should encourage and support a realistic estimate of the situation by anyone whose death is approaching. If someone who might still be able to make a free choice is in danger of death but not aware of it, those who know the true state of affairs should make sure he or she is informed. This of course calls for prudence and gentleness, and is best done by someone close to the individual. But it is a grave matter to allow anyone enjoying the use of reason to die without an opportunity to prepare for death, and an even graver matter to mislead someone about something so important.

Germain Grisez, *Living a Christian Life*, 240

FOR PERSONAL CONSIDERATION

1. Do I fear to speak about death? Prayerfully ask God both for courage and prudence. Ask the Holy Spirit to guide what you say and when to speak.

2. Send a card of encouragement to someone who is ill and include a Scripture quote that will help him to see his present suffering from a godly perspective (for example: 2 Tim 2 or Rom 5).

CHAPTER 21

Is Grieving Compatible with a Catholic Approach?

If we are to have an eternal outlook and if therein we are to find perspective, joy, and peace, should we grieve when someone dies? And if grieving is acceptable or appropriate, what is a Catholic approach?

For 26 years of my working career I was employed by various Catholic cemetery organizations. The number of burials per year ranged from about 2000 to almost 5000 a year. It is fair to say that, in some way, I was involved with over 70,000 deaths!

Despite the amount of experience, I am still hesitant to make too many generalizations about death and grieving because each of those 70,000 deaths involved unique individuals, situations, and responses. Aspects such as how a person died, past history, culture, ethnicity, personality, and temperament all play a part in how a person handles the death of a loved one.

Nonetheless, I can with confidence make one observation. Those with strong faith generally handled the death of a loved one better than those with weak or minimal faith. Those with strong faith tend to put death in the correct perspective. They know that God is on the throne and that His intentions will prevail — suffering has meaning; the resurrected Lord gives hope. Death, for the strong believer, is seen as the doorway to eternity, and eternity is full of promise. Yet individuals with deep faith may grieve deeply, experience profoundly a sense of loss and they may experience anger — even anger against God. And they may experience these emotions deeply.

In fact, the death of a loved one may be a time that tests their faith and their relationship with God. Even those whom we see as being saintly and heroic in living their faith can be shaken by death. It is enlightening to read *A Grief Observed* by C.S. Lewis. Here a man of strong faith looks soberly at the trials of losing the person dearest to him. It was a terrible and painful experience.

Also, if you read the Psalms, such as Psalms 6, 13, and 55, you will see how the writer of these prayers struggled with the concept of death. Considering "the terrors of death," the psalmist writes: "My heart is in anguish within me, . . . Fear and trembling come upon me" (Ps 55:4-5). Or ponder the words of Psalm 116 where the psalmist considers the "snares of death." He admits that there were tears in his eyes, his feet stumbled, and he "suffered distress and anguish" (Ps 116:3, 8).

But even though C.S. Lewis, the psalmist, and others with faith and an eternal perspective may struggle and even wrestle with God (cf. Gen 32:24-29), they ultimately find blessing, acceptance, and peace. The psalmist also writes: "Even though I walk through the valley of the shadow of death, I fear no evil; for thou art with me; thy rod and thy staff, they comfort me" (Ps 23:4). It makes no difference whether the death that affects the writer of this Psalm is his own or that of another, he finds comfort in God. He knows that the *faithful* departed "shall dwell in the house of the LORD for ever" (Ps 23:6).

Catholics with an eternal perspective and a confident faith in a loving God grieve, but they do not despair. They struggle, but they are not overcome. They are tried, but God is not found wanting. In fact, for many people of faith, the necessity of facing death can be, and often is, an opportunity to grow closer to God, to better rely upon Him, and to find hope, regardless of the outward circumstances. They see this life as a transition to the next. They can say with St. Paul: "we have this treasure in earthen vessels, to show that the transcendent power belongs to God and not to us. We are afflicted in every way, but not crushed; perplexed, but not driven to despair; persecuted, but not forsaken; struck down, but not destroyed" (2 Cor 4:7-9).

But what of those who have some faith and are somewhat religious? These individuals believe in God, but that belief has little impact on how they live their lives. It may be that their faith was passed on to them by parents or through the culture. They may do their natural best to live a moral life. But faith has not taken real root in their lives. It is these individuals who tend to be overwhelmed by the death of a loved one. Certainly their reaction will correspond to the circumstances of the death. The passing of an elderly grandmother who lived a full and blessed life may not impact them to the same degree as the death of a child who is tragically killed in a car accident. However, the difference is often one of degree rather than of understanding.

They will tend to see death as grossly unjust because it appears to break a relationship. They will focus on what could have been, but wasn't, and now can't be. When they experience grief, a sense of loss, and angry feelings, they tend to be overwhelmed because they have no frame of reference in which to deal with these feelings. Their predominant focus is this world and this life. They may have a belief in heaven, but it is this earthly life that is most real to them. Lacking the perspective of the eternal, they are at a loss to bring understanding to the reality of death. These are the individuals who identify death as "unfair." Their anger can lead to bitterness. Their sense of loss can lead to feelings of loneliness and abandonment. Their grief can consume them and lead them to despair.

Death for us can be like a bucket of cold water to the face. For some, that is a grace to awaken them so that they can reevaluate their own lives and search for answers that really address the problem of death and mortality. Others see it as an insult and believe that life has treated them rudely. They may allow life to sweep them along in its tide and so "deal" with death by getting on with living, but they do not find an answer that satisfies the spirit. Their shallow faith becomes even less of a factor in their lives.

It is important to note that some individuals with firm faith will experience some of the same stages of grief as a person with minimal faith, perhaps even to a greater degree. Some readers of this book may be struggling now with these same emotions. But, like C.S. Lewis or the psalmist, all struggles, when consistently given to Christ, will eventually be victories — if not in this life then certainly in the next. Pain and feelings of loss may remain, but hope will always bring perspective.

We can always trust the words of Christ given to us through St. Paul: "We are more than conquerors through him who loved us. For I am sure that neither death, nor life, nor angels, nor principalities, nor things present, nor things to come, nor powers, nor height, nor depth, nor anything else in all creation, will be able to separate us from the love of God in Christ Jesus our Lord" (Rom 8:37-39).

Good Grief

The writer of Ecclesiastes tells us that there is "a time to die ... a time to weep ... [and] a time to mourn" (Eccles 3:2, 4). When Jesus arrives at the tomb of his friend Lazarus, Scripture tells us "Jesus wept" (Jn 11:35). The death of someone close to Him was, apparently, a right "time to weep." If it is appropriate for the Son of God, it is appropriate for us.

To experience feelings of loss at the death of a loved one is a very human experience. The separation and accompanying pain and loss caused by death was not part of God's original intent for man. It was, and is, a consequence of the fall. It was, and is, part of the very temporary victory of Satan. We can experience just anger when confronted with death for it is part of a fallen condition. But there is also an understanding that the "sting of death" has been taken away (cf. 1 Cor. 15:56). The Christian knows that Christ has conquered death, but also knows that it is "the last enemy to be destroyed" (1 Cor 15:26).

Consider the words of St. Paul to the Thessalonians: "But we would not have you ignorant, brethren, concerning those who are asleep, that you may not grieve as others do who have no hope. For since we believe that Jesus died and rose again, even so, through Jesus, God will bring with him those who have fallen asleep" (1 Thess 4:13-14). Paul does not forbid grieving for the deceased, rather he says that the grieving of a Christian should be suffused with hope. Pain is pain and it is part of our human condition in this fallen world. If I hit my thumb with a hammer, I feel pain. If my wife dies, I will experience grief — the pain of loss. But hitting my thumb should not make me give up on the construction project, and the death of my wife should not lead me to despair of the hope I have in Christ.

Mourning can be a means of sharing in the pain of another and a worthy way to encourage another. Sirach tells us: "Give graciously to all the living, and withhold not kindness from the dead. Do not fail those who weep, but mourn with those who mourn" (Sir 7:33-34).

In our human condition we experience the effects of our fallen nature. Pain, sorrow, loss, and grief are a part of who we are. To share that with others is a means of encouragement and support. Yet spiritual vision sees, even in the midst of struggle, that Christ has conquered death. Death is but the final sparks from a dying fire. This world is passing away and "death shall be no more, neither shall there be mourning nor crying nor pain any more, for the former things have passed away" (Rev 21:4). We await the full manifestation of eternal glory. It is then that every tear will be wiped away.

Jesus wept.

Jn 11:35

> Christian hope places a completely different character on the face of death. For death becomes now the hour of our encounter with the Holy of Holies, Jesus Christ, in whose heart the fullness of the Godhead dwells. Death means the encounter at last with the God-Man, the Beloved of our soul, the One for whom we have been created.
>
> Dietrich von Hildebrand
> *Jaws of Death: Gate of Heaven*, 89

FOR PERSONAL CONSIDERATION

1. If you are struggling with grief, it is a struggle that you do not need to fight alone. Prayer and the sacraments, especially Eucharist and the sacrament of Reconciliation, are indispensable. Consult a priest and ask for his guidance. Also, consider joining a grief support group or seeing a professional counselor. If you broke your arm or contracted an illness, while continuing to pray for God's strength and healing, you would also see a doctor and take the medicine prescribed. If the emotions associated with grief seem to be overwhelming you, professional assistance and medication, coupled with prayer and the sacraments, can be a great help.

2. Having completed this book, what resolutions will you make? Review the books in the bibliography. Is there a title that you want to read to further deepen your understanding and faith?

Prayers

Prayer to St. Joseph

Oh glorious St. Joseph, model of all who are devoted to labor, obtain for me the grace to work in a spirit of penance in expiation of my many sins; to work conscientiously by placing love of duty above my inclinations; to gratefully and joyously deem it an honor to employ and to develop by labor the gifts I have received from God, to work methodically, peacefully, and in moderation and patience, without ever shrinking from it through weariness or difficulty to work; above all, with purity of intention and unselfishness, having unceasingly before my eyes death and the account I have to render of time lost, talents unused, good not done, and vain complacency in success, so baneful to the work of God. All for Jesus, all for Mary, all to imitate thee, O Patriarch St. Joseph! This shall be my motto for life and eternity. Amen.

Pope St. Pius X

Prayer for Perseverance

Lord Jesus, Scripture tells me that Your "face was set toward Jerusalem" (Lk 9:53). Nothing could stop You from facing Your trial, crucifixion, and death. With courage and perseverance You accepted Your Father's will. Help me to embrace Your will for me. Help me to see my own death not as a tragedy or as something to be feared, but rather as a part of Your will for me. Grant me the hope, the courage, and the perseverance that sustained You through the difficult times of your life. May I share in Your resurrection and, at my death, come into the eternal home that Your love and mercy have prepared for me.

Regis J. Flaherty

Prayer to Christ the King

O Jesus Christ, I acknowledge You as universal King. All that has been made has been created for You. Exercise all Your rights over me. I renew my baptismal vows, renouncing Satan, his pomps, and his works; and I promise to live as a good Christian. In particular do I pledge myself to labor, to the best of my ability, for the triumph of the rights of God and Your Church.

Divine Heart of Jesus, to You I offer my poor services, laboring that all hearts may acknowledge Your Sacred Kingship, and that thus the reign of Your peace be established throughout the whole universe. Amen.

Adapted from: *My Catholic Faith: A Manual of Religion*
by Most Rev. Louis Laravoire Morrow, S.T.D.
My Mission House, 1965

Prayer for a Right Perspective

O Holy Spirit, enlighten my mind that death may not be my enemy, that I may not fear it in an unseemly way for a Christian, that I may not run from death, so that when death comes and takes those dear to me, I may welcome their release from this valley of tears although I am myself deeply moved and even deprived by their departure from this world. Let me know that death reminds each of us of the infinite reality of life with you. Let me see all things in the perspective of death and everlasting life. And let me not be filled with grief either at the anticipation of my own death or the experience of the death of those dear to me. Rather, strengthen my faith, that in the midst of this changing world, I may always come closer to you, who never changes and who awaits me and those dear to me together with the Father and the Son in life everlasting.

Fr. Benedict J. Groeschel
Arise from Darkness: When Life Doesn't Make Sense, 130

Prayer as Death Draws Near

Lord... help us to die according to your will, perhaps in fear, perhaps in absolute pain, perhaps in our sleep, or experiencing death drawing near hour by hour, but in any case in such a way that we do not forsake the thought of you, but know that every death, even the dark one, is your possession and has died in you on the Cross. Help us to die as believers, that our faith may also shine on the others present at our dying, that it may be of help to them and later, perhaps, also be of comfort to them when their own hour comes. Lord, make your presence known to all who are left behind; help them to overcome their grief; be with them to the end of their days. Amen.

Adrienne von Speyr
First Look at Adrienne von Speyr, 213-214

Prayer for the Forgotten Souls in Purgatory

O merciful God, take pity on those souls who have no particular friends and intercessors to recommend them to You. Spare them, O Lord, and remember Your mercy. Let not the souls which You have created be parted from You, their Creator. They are Your work, and though they have sinned, they have been redeemed by You. Vouchsafe, therefore, to look upon them and to deliver them from the intolerable pain of absence from You, the Light and Love of all Your creatures.

Psalm 90

LORD, thou hast been our dwelling place in all generations.
Before the mountains were brought forth,
    or ever thou hadst formed the earth and the world,
    from everlasting to everlasting thou art God.
Thou turnest man back to the dust,
    and sayest, "Turn back, O children of men!"
For a thousand years in thy sight
    are but as yesterday when it is past,
    or as a watch in the night.

Thou dost sweep men away; they are like a dream,
    like grass which is renewed in the morning:
in the morning it flourishes and is renewed;
    in the evening it fades and withers.
For we are consumed by thy anger;
    by thy wrath we are overwhelmed.
Thou hast set our iniquities before thee,
    our secret sins in the light of thy countenance.
For all our days pass away under thy wrath,
    our years come to an end like a sigh.
The years of our life are threescore and ten,
    or even by reason of strength fourscore;
yet their span is but toil and trouble;
    they are soon gone, and we fly away.
Who considers the power of thy anger,
    and thy wrath according to the fear of thee?
So teach us to number our days
    that we may get a heart of wisdom.
Return, O LORD! How long?
    Have pity on thy servants!
Satisfy us in the morning with thy steadfast love,
    that we may rejoice and be glad all our days.
Make us glad as many days as thou hast afflicted us,
    and as many years as we have seen evil.
Let thy work be manifest to thy servants,
    and thy glorious power to their children.
Let the favor of the Lord our God be upon us,
    and establish thou the work of our hands upon us,
    yea, the work of our hands establish thou it.

BIBLIOGRAPHY

Ball, Ann. *Catholic Book of the Dead*. Huntington, IN: Our Sunday Visitor, 2002.

Bellarmine, Robert. *Live Well, Die Well*. Manchester, NH: Sophia Press, 1998.

Curley, Terence P., D. Min. *Six Steps for Managing Loss*. New York: Alba House, 1997.

D'Arcy, M.C., S.J. *Death and Life*. Fort Collins, CO: Roger A. McCaffrey Publishing.

Drummey, James J. et al. *Catholicism & Life: Commandments & Sacraments*. Norwood, MA: C.R. Publications, 1996.

Dubruiel, Michael. *The How-To Book of the Mass*. Huntington, IN: Our Sunday Visitor, 2002.

Flaherty, Regis J. *Catholic Customs: A Fresh Look at Traditional Practices*. Cincinnati: Saint Anthony Messenger/Servant Books, 2002.

Flaherty, Regis J. and Aquilina, Mike. *The How to Book of Catholic Devotions*. Huntington, IN: Our Sunday Visitor, 2000.

Goodier, Most Rev. Alban, S.J. *The Meaning of Life*. Fort Collins, CO: Roger A. McCaffrey Publishing.

Groeschel, Benedict J., C.F.R. *Arise from Darkness*. San Francisco: Ignatius Press, 1995.

Halligan, Nicholas. *The Sacraments and Their Celebration*. New York: Alba House, 1986.

Hahn, Scott. *First Comes Love: Finding Your Family in the Church and the Trinity*. New York: Doubleday, 2002.

Kreeft, Peter. *Everything You Ever Wanted to Know About Heaven but Never Dreamed of Asking*. San Francisco: Ignatius Press, 1990.

_____. *Love Is Stronger than Death*. San Francisco: Ignatius Press, 1992.

_____. *Fundamentals of the Faith*. San Francisco: Ignatius Press, 1988.

Lockwood, Robert P. *A Faith for Grown-Ups: A Midlife Conversation About What Really Matters*. Chicago: Loyola Press, 2004.

Martin, Ralph. *Hungry for God: Practical Help in Personal Prayer*. San Francisco: Ignatius Press, 2000.

Miller, Rev. J. Michael, C.S.B. *Praying for the Dead: A Holy and Pious Thought*. Huntington, IN: Our Sunday Visitor, 1994.

Mork, Dom Wulstan, O.S.B. *Transformed by Grace*. Cincinnati: Saint Anthony Messenger/Servant Books, 2004.

Neuhaus, Richard John, editor. *The Eternal Pity*. Notre Dame, IN: University of Notre Dame Press, 2000.

Schonborn, Christoph, trans. Brian McNeil, C.R.V. *From Death to Life*. San Francisco: Ignatius Press, 1995.

Sheed, F.J. *Theology and Sanity*. New York: Sheed & Ward, 1946.

von Hildebrand, Dietrich. *Jaws of Death: Gate of Heaven*. Manchester, NH: Sophia Press, 1981.

von Speyr, Adrienne, trans. Graham Harrison. *The Mystery of Death*. San Francisco: Ignatius Press, 1988.

NOTES

Preface
[1] Benedict J. Groeschel, C.F.R., *Arise from Darkness: When Life Doesn't Make Sense* (San Francisco: Ignatius Press, 1995), 123.

Introduction
[2] Benedict J. Groeschel, C.F.R., *Arise from Darkness: When Life Doesn't Make Sense* (San Francisco: Ignatius Press, 1995), 120-121.

[3] St. Thérèse of Lisieux, *The Autobiography of Saint Thérèse of Lisieux, the Little Flower of Jesus,* translated by Rev. Thomas N. Taylor (New York: P.J. Kenedy & Sons, 1920), 72.

Chapter 1
[4] All of the statistics in this section are taken from an October 2003 survey by the Barna Group. Findings were published as "Americans Describe Their Views About Life After Death" at www.barna.org. Barna Research Group, Ltd., 5528 Everglades Street, Ventura, CA 93003.

[5] Peter Kreeft, *Love Stronger than Death* (San Francisco: Ignatius Press, 1992), 55.

[6] Adrienne von Spyr, *The Mystery of Death*, translated by Graham Harrison (San Francisco: Ignatius Press, 1988), 8.

[7] Ibid., 30.

[8] Peter Kreeft, *Love Stronger than Death*, 23.

[9] Second Vatican Council, *Dei Verbum*, 5.

Chapter 2
[10] Read Chapter 6 for explanation of the reuniting of soul and body at the end of this world.

[11] See Mt 5:22, 29; 10:18; 13:42, 50; Mk 9:43-48.

Chapter 3
[12] See Chapter 19 for a discussion of the particular judgment.

[13] For the distinction between "venial" and "mortal" sins read CCC 1854 through 1864.

[14] Hans Urs von Bathasar, *The Christian State in Life*, translated by Sister Mary Frances McCarthy (Ignatius Press: San Francisco, 1983), 127.

[15] Frank Sheed, *Death into Life* (New York: Arena Letters, 1977), 132.

[16] Quoted in *The Navarre Bible: Corinthians,* commentary by members of the Faculty of Theology of the University of Navarre, trans. Michael Adams (Four Courts Press: Dublin, Ireland, 1991), 62.

[17] Benedict J. Groeschel, C.F.R., *Arise from Darkness: When Life Doesn't Make Sense,* 114.

Chapter 4
[18] See Eph 4:12, 16; 1 Cor 10:16; 12:27, Rom 7:4; 12:4.

[19] Jn 15:1-6.

[20] *Webster's New World Dictionary of American English,* Third College Edition, Victoria Neufeldt, ed. (New York, NY: Simon and Schuster, Inc., 1986).

[21] We can effectively pray for the members of the Church Militant and Suffering. Those who are in heaven no longer need our prayers since they now enjoy the beatific vision and could want nothing further. Prayer for those in purgatory will be discussed in the next chapter.

[22] Taken from *Day by Day with Mary,* John E. Rotelle, O.S.A. ed., (Villanova, PA: Augustine Press, 2001), 303.

[23] It is Jesus who saves us, but it was Mary's "yes" that brought the Savior to the world.

[24] *Dulia* is the Latin word that indicates the honor we accord to the saints in heaven. *Hyperdulia* is the veneration that we give to Mary as the saint most worthy of honor. Only God is worthy of worship which is identified by the Latin word *latria.*

Chapter 5
[25] From the first preface for funeral liturgy.

[26] From the *Order of Christian Funerals* (OCF), translation by ICEL, 1989.

[27] Concupiscence is "a desire of the lower appetite contrary to reason. . . . [It is] desires contrary to the real good and order of reason." *The Catholic Encyclopedia, Volume IV*, Robert Appleton Company, 1908. Online Edition Copyright 2003 at NewAdvent.com.

Chapter 6
[28] See CCC 1257-1261.

Chapter 7
[29] See Mt 10:12-24; 16:27; 24; Mk 8:38; 13; Lk 8:26; 21; and most of the book of Revelation.

Chapter 9

[30] Germain Grisez, *The Way of the Lord Jesus: Christian Moral Principles* (Quincy, IL: Franciscan Press, 1983) Chapter 31, Question F.

Chapter 10

[31] In addition to water baptism, there are two other forms of Baptism recognized by the Church. The first is Baptism of blood where an unbaptized individual gives his life for the faith. Baptism of desire, the other form, occurs when an individual who desires Baptism dies before actual Baptism. An example would be a catechumen who dies before water baptism. The Church also recognizes that someone who has not heard the gospel but, who "seeks the truth and does the will of God in accordance with his understanding of it, can be saved" (CCC 1260). In this case the Church sees that such a person "would have *desired Baptism explicitly* if they had known its necessity" (CCC 1261). The Church works to see that all men are baptized. Christ taught her that Baptism is necessary for salvation. And he commanded the Church to baptize for salvation. Yet She does not judge the salvation of individuals. *"God has bound salvation to the sacrament of Baptism, but he himself is not bound by his sacraments"* (CCC 1257, emphasis in the original).

Chapter 11

[32] The reference here could easily be the entire New Testament. Lk 6:12-49 is a good place to begin reading.

[33] Germain Grisez, *Living a Christian Life* (Quincy, IL: Franciscan Press, 1993), 461.

[34] Adrienne von Speyr, *The Holy Mass* (San Francisco: Ignatius Press, 1999), 76.

Chapter 12

[35] Scott Hahn, *First Comes Love* (New York: Doubleday, 2002), 68-73.

[36] Ibid., 69.

[37] Second Vatican Council, Dogmatic Constitution *Lumen Gentium*, 5.

[38] Congregation for the Doctrine of the Faith, *Dominus Iesus* (On the Unicity and Salvific Universality of Jesus Christ and the Church), June 2000, 18.

[39] The Paraclete is "a designation of the Holy Ghost . . . [that] has been variously translated 'advocate', 'intercessor', 'teacher', 'helper'. See *The Catholic Encyclopedia* 1911, available at http://www.newadvent.org/cathen/11469a.htm.

Chapter 13

[40] If a spouse dies, another valid marriage is possible, but you can only be in one valid marriage at a time.

[41] Given on Sunday, June 5, 1988 when the Holy Father celebrated Mass in Reggio Emilia.

[42] "*Panis Angelicus*" is a hymn written by St. Thomas Aquinas for the Feast of Corpus Christi. This is a translation of the hymn by John David Chambers (1805-1893).

> Thus Angels' Bread is made
> the Bread of man today:
> the Living Bread from heaven
> with figures dost away:
> O wondrous gift indeed!
> the poor and lowly may
> upon their Lord and Master feed
>
> Thee, therefore, we implore,
> O Godhead, One in Three,
> so may Thou visit us
> as we now worship Thee;
> and lead us on Thy way,
> That we at last may see
> the light wherein Thou dwellest aye.

[43] For a more in-depth discussion of the sacraments see my book, *Catholic Customs: A Fresh Look at Traditional Practices*, Servant books, 2002.

Chapter 14

[44] See also Phil 2:16 and Gal 2:2.

[45] I have written two other books, which I offer for your consideration: *The How to Book of Catholic Devotions* and *Catholic Customs: A Fresh Look at Tradition Practices*. More information on these books can be found in the bibliography at the end of this book.

[46] See CCC 131-133.

Chapter 15

[47] See Mt 8:26, 28:5,10; Mk 4:40; Lk 1:13, 2:10, 5:10, 12:32; Jn 6:20; Acts 18:9, 27:24. See also Heb 13:6.

Chapter 17

[48] *Code of Canon Law*, 847.

Chapter 18

[49] "A Christian rite ... comprises the manner of performing all services for the worship of God and the sanctification of men." *Catholic Encyclopedia*, 1912. Definition can be found at http://www.newadvent.org/cathen/13064b.htm.

[50] Separation is only physical. We remain connected to the departed in the Communion of Saints. See Chapter 4.

[51] Violet and black vestments are also permitted. See the "General Introduction" to *The Order of Christian Funerals*, 39.

[52] "Sacramentals: Sacred signs, whether objects (e.g., scapulars, holy water) or actions (e.g., blessings), possessing a likeness to the sacraments and whose effects are obtained by the prayer of the Church (Can. 1166). The sacraments were instituted by Christ and effect grace by virtue of themselves; the sacramentals are instituted by the Church and impart grace according to the disposition of the recipients and the intercession of the Church. CCC 1667-1676" Peter M. J. Stavinskas, *Catholic Dictionary* (Huntington, IN: Our Sunday Visitor, 2002).

[53] This may also occur at the church or funeral home if the body will not be accompanied to the place of burial. It may also occur at the crematory if the body is to be cremated.

Chapter 19

[54] See Chapters 2 and 3.

[55] *Baltimore Catechism* #1, question 6.

[56] "Fear," *The Catholic Encyclopedia*, Volume VI, 1909. It can be found at http://www.newadvent.org/cathen/06021a.htm.

[57] John A. Hardon, *The Catholic Catechism* (New York: Doubleday, 1981), 205.

Chapter 20

[58] Not his real name.

[59] Vatican II, *Decree on the Apostolate of the Laity*, 1, 2.

[60] Ibid., 1, 3.